EDUCATION, ARTS, AND MORALITY
Creative Journeys

PATH IN PSYCHOLOGY

Published in Cooperation with Publications for the
Advancement of Theory and History in Psychology (PATH)

Series Editors:
David Bakan, *York University*
John M. Broughton, *Teachers College, Columbia University*
Robert W. Rieber, *John Hay College, CUNY, and Columbia University*
Howard Gruber, *University of Geneva*

EDUCATION, ARTS, AND MORALITY
Creative Journeys

Edited by

Doris B. Wallace
New York, New York

Kluwer Academic/Plenum Publishers
New York, Boston, Dordrecht, London, Moscow

Library of Congress Cataloging-in-Publication Data

Education, arts, and morality : creative journeys / edited by Doris B. Wallace.
    p.   cm. – (PATH in psycology)
    Includes bibliographical references and index.
    ISBN 0-306-48670-9 – ISBN 0-306-48671-7 (ebook)
    1. Creative ability.   2. Moral education.   3. Creative ability–Case studies.
    I. Wallace, Doris B.   II. Series.
    BF408.E37 2005
    153.3′5–dc22   2004048557

ISBN 0-306-48670-9

© 2005 by Kluwer Academic/Plenum Publishers, New York
233 Spring Street, New York, New York 10013

http://www.kluweronline.com

10 9 8 7 6 5 4 3 2 1

A C.I.P. record for this book is available from the Library of Congress

Permissions for books published in Europe: permissions@wkap.nl
Permissions for books published in the United States of America: permissions@wkap.com

Printed in the United States of America

For Howard

CONTRIBUTORS

Richard Brower, Wagner College, Staten Island, NY

Sara Davis, Rosemont College, Rosemont, PA

Michael Hanchett Hanson, Teachers College, Columbia University, New York, NY

Helen Haste, University of Bath, Bath, UK

Yeh Hsueh, University of Memphis, Memphis, TN

David Lavery, Middle Tennessee State University, Murfreesboro, TN

Susan Rostan, Hofstra University, Hempstead, NY

Laura Tahir, Garden State Youth Correctional Facility, Yardville, NJ

PREFACE

Howard E. Gruber's evolving systems approach to creativity has, in various ways, influenced all the contributors to this volume. A central tenet in Gruber's approach is that, in considering the creative thought and work of a preeminently creative person, it is the person's uniqueness that brings him or her to our attention in the first place. The discovery, novelty, breakthrough or change of paradigm represented by the person's ideas and products is unlike those of anyone else. It follows that in order to deepen our understanding of the development of the person's work, a case study is the best approach. Lavery, Hanchett Hanson, and Brower each use the case study to explore an aspect of the work of a highly creative individual.

David Lavery studies the essays and poetry of the American anthropologist, historian of science and writer Loren Eiseley and the latter's goal to feel at home when he is away from home. Lavery discusses some central metaphors in Eiseley's thought and draws parallels between Odysseus' homeward journey and Eiseley's professional and personal one.

Michael Hanchett Hanson's study focuses on the role of irony in George Bernard Shaw's writings about World War I, the Great War. Hanchett Hanson shows how Shaw's use of irony contributed to his creativity and reflected his moral passion.

Richard Brower uses the social-psychological theory of social comparison to trace the development of van Gogh as an artist. Brower's study contradicts the prevalent idea that the highly creative individual is a solitary figure who works alone, cut off from the world.

Sara Davis describes her study of the relationship between reader and text when the text is a romance novel. She discusses the heavy influence of broad cultural norms concerning women and romance, but also shows how readers who initially had a very negative attitude to romance novels, constructed new meanings of the text once they began to read. Davis' interest in social context is indebted to Gruber, who believed that examination of the effects of the social milieu is essential in the study of individual creativity.

Several authors mention Gruber's *Network of Enterprise* which is a theoretical construct that also provides a methodological technique to map a person's enterprises over time. An enterprise is a purposeful activity of some duration (weeks, months, years) which consists of projects, tasks, and products. Gruber used the *Network* idea in the course of developing his approach to the study of creative work. Laura Tahir, who directs the psychological services in a prison, applies this tool to her work with two members of a group of young incarcerated men. Together with her use of narrative therapy—whose main focus is for those in therapy to "re-story" their lives—Tahir discusses the potential effects of her program on the future lives of the participants.

Susan Rostan uses Gruber's work on morality and creativity as a take-off point to examine extraordinary moral behavior in children of elementary and high school age and traces aspects of its developmental course across these age groups. Rostan includes teachers' perceptions of the extraordinary moral behavior they witnessed and discusses the importance of teachers' potential roles in the development of such behavior among their students.

Yeh Hsueh takes up the method of *Critical Exploration* in education. He traces the origins of this approach to Jean Piaget's development of the "clinical method" as a way of interviewing and working with children. Hsueh carefully describes the evolution of the approach in the 20th century and its current use by Eleanor Duckworth as a way of eliciting maximum participation and creative thinking in the classroom.

Helen Haste uses a broad brush to examine questions of how best to educate young people for moral and civic responsibility. Her examination includes research studies in Western and Eastern Europe, North and South America, and Asia. She emphasizes the importance of taking changing political, social, and psychological world events (such as the entry of environmentalism into the public domain) into consideration in making decisions about curriculum. Haste discusses broad theoretical issues, questions about participation and practice, as well as the meaning of responsibility at the individual level.

It is easy to see in these brief descriptions that the essays in this volume owe a collective debt to Howard Gruber—from an abstract-idea level to the concrete adoption of method. At the same time, it is striking how many of the contributors are presenting work in areas never explored by Gruber. This, perhaps, attests to the generativity and flexibility of Gruber's theory.

Doris B. Wallace
New York

ACKNOWLEDGEMENTS

As the editor, I thank the contributors for what they have written and for their patience. In addition there are those who helped at various stages: Robert Rieber, who had the initial idea for the book, John Broughton, who was helpful and always kind, Margery Franklin and Edna Shapiro, whose good judgment has been invaluable. All these people made suggestions, offered valuable criticism and were encouraging for which I am deeply grateful. I also wish to acknowledge my family for their general tolerance of my inaccessibility at various stages.

CONTENTS

ROOTED IN THE ABSENCE OF PLACE
THE ODYSSEY OF LOREN EISELEY

David Lavery

There is a Bible in every wanderer's bedroom,
where there might better be the Odyssey.
                    J. Hillman (1975, p. 28).

And I asked: "You mean death, then?"
"Yes," the voice said, "Die into what the earth
requires of you."
W. Berry, "Song in a Year of Catastrophe" (1984, p. 40).

We must take the feeling of being at home into exile.
We must be rooted in the absence of place.
                    Simone Weil (1977, p. 356)

PERSONAL KNOWLEDGE

In his essay "Concerning the Poet," Rainer Maria Rilke (1978) seeks to provide an analogy for the position of the poet in the existing world by describing a boat which he once traveled, manned by oarsman pulling steadfastly against the current of a great river. Although the crew counts aloud to keep time, Rilke tells us, they remain uncommunicative, constantly reverting to the "watchful gaze of an animal," and their individual voices fail to become articulate. But at the front of the boat, on the right side, one individual does achieve expression. He sings, suddenly and irregularly, as if to guide the work of the crew, often when the other rowers are exuberantly engaged only in their task and unmindful of all else. He seems, Rilke notes, little influenced by the rest of the crew who sit behind him; it is, rather, the "pure movement of his feeling when it met the open distance" (p. 66) that truly concerns him and inspires him. His song springs out of the counterpoise which centers the forward thrust of the vessel and the opposing force of the river, and although the boat moves successfully through the water, there remains nevertheless a residue of something "that could not be overcome (was not susceptible of being overcome p. 66);" and that residue the singer in the front of the boat

> transmuted into a series of long floating sounds, detached in space, which each appropriated to himself. While those about him were always occupied with the most immediate actuality and the overcoming of it, his voice maintained contact with the farthest distance, linking us with it until we felt the power of its attraction (p. 66).

This Man is the Poet

Loren Eiseley (1907–1977) was undeniably such a poet, a writer whose voice and eye maintained "contact with the farthest distance" of the species' journey into time, the magnitude and pathos of which he had come to know only due to the longing of science and its revelatory power, without, however, abandoning either the personalities of authentic poetic utterance or the burden of the past and the pathos of memory. Eiseley was a professor of anthropology (a specialist in physical anthropology), formerly chairman of the department at the University of Pennsylvania, Provost of the University, Curator of Early Man at its museum, and the author of numerous scholarly articles and fourteen books—ten prose and four poetry (four of which were published posthumously)—reflections, both scholarly and personal, on subjects like evolution, the natural world, anthropology and archaeology, the history of science, and literature. But he became a professional scholar and academic only by chance.

As his autobiographical writing reveals—and in a sense all of his work is autobiographical—throughout his life he believed that he was always about to be snatched away from his ordinary, tame world into a "world of violence" far removed from the sober pursuits of the university life for which he felt only a dubious affinity. Eiseley came to intellectual ventures relatively late in life and in a roundabout way after a youth spent, in part, as a hobo during the Great Depression. His first book, The Immense Journey (1957), which launched his career as a literary naturalist, was not published until he was nearly fifty, and as a glance at a bibliography of his work will reveal, he maintained his career as a writer afterwards only with some difficulty. At times, in the twenty years of his life that remained, he found it impossible to publish at all. From 1960 to 1969 he did not produce a single book.

That he ever came to write the kind of books that he did—which have been described as occupying a kind of no man's land between literature and science—came about almost by accident. Commissioned to do an essay on evolution for a scholarly journal in the 1950s, Eiseley had this project well under way when the journal backed out of the agreement. Although he was suffering from temporary deafness at the time (see "The Ghost World" in All the Strange Hours [1975a]), he nevertheless decided to attempt instead something more literary—an out-of-fashion personal essay. The Immense Journey (1957) was the eventual result, and with it was born his experimentation with a form he liked to call the "concealed essay," in which "personal anecdote was allowed to bring under observation thoughts of a more purely scientific nature..." (1975a, p. 177). The essayist, Eiseley believed, unlike the painter, "sees as his own eye dictates"; "he peers out upon modern pictures and transposes them in some totemic ceremony" (1975a, pp. 154–55).

Eiseley had long contemplated a full-fledged career as a man of letters, not as a scientist. As he himself has told us (1975a), it was only after an almost archetypal encounter with an English teacher, who thought one of his papers too well written to be his own, that he turned finally to science, his second love, for his primary career. "There are subjects in which I have remained dwarfed all of my adult life because of the ill-considered blow of someone nursing pent-up aggressions, or because of words more violent in their end effects than blows," he explains in The Night Country (1971, p. 201). English, and consequently creative writing, were for him such subjects. Yet, as Carlisle (1983) points out in a biographical study of the author's development as a writer, Eiseley was a published poet and short story writer as early as the 1930s, long before he was a scholar and a scientist, and in a sense he remained a creative writer who discovered in the insights of science the substance of great art.

Science, the biologist Haldane once argued, is, in fact, more stimulating than the classics of literature, but the fact is not widely known for the simple reason that scientific men as a class are devoid of any perception of literary form (Wilson, 1978, pp. 201–202). As Eiseley learned how to apply his essentially literary sensibility to the raw materials of science of anthropology—an intellectual activity which, as Levi-Strauss observes, "rejoins at one extreme the history of the world and at the other the history of myself [unveiling] the shared motivations of one and the other at the same moment" (1955, p. 51)—his grasp of literary form, his understanding of the expressive potential of the concealed essay, however, became more and more sure. But his fusion of science and art brought about more than a mastery of technique. In his own art of the essay, Eiseley interwove the story of an individual life—his own—with the story of life's immense journey so tightly that, looking back over his work as a whole it is difficult to say which was warp and which woof.

In the tradition of Montaigne, Eiseley knew that the success or failure of his essays as art depended primarily on his presentation of self: "The self and its minute adventures may be interesting... but only if one is utterly, nakedly honest and does not pontificate" (1975a, p. 178). Yet, as he himself admits in his preface to Notes of an Alchemist (a book of poems that he refused to publish until retirement, at least partly out of fear of the criticism it would bring upon him), to be "nakedly honest" about the inner life is not considered to be "normal science" within the tradition in which Eiseley's professional life transpired: "the austerities of the scientific profession," he noted, "leave most of us silent upon our inner lives" (1972, p. 11). On his own inner life, however, Eiseley remained anything but silent. His injunction to his readers in All the Strange Hours—"My anatomy lies bare. Read if you wish or pass on" (1975a, p. 219)—appears in an autobiography gripping in its candor, and the same might be said for all his works. Consequently, he has, by telling the story of a life grounded in science, bequeathed to us a body of work in which science becomes a means of expressing the "personal knowledge" of the world which Michael Polanyi (1962) has insisted it always has been, despite the bravura of its false show of unimpeachable objectivity. And yet Eiseley's voice has not really been heard, nor his achievement as a writer truly appreciated. In a time like our own, still entranced by the temptations of positivism, his imaginary genius has prevented his work from being as yet influential.

In Darwin Retried, Norman Macbeth (1971), critical of the predominance of Darwinian thought in the development of evolutionary theory, asks that evolutionists admit their secret doubt of the validity of Darwinism to the public; he petitions them to make a full disclosure. It is no small part of the achievement of Loren Eiseley that he made such a disclosure. His prose and poetry present, however, much more than his questioning of the Darwinian world view, which on one occasion he described as "too simplistic for belief" (1975a, p. 245). They reveal as well Eiseley's doubts about the nature and meaning of science itself, the doubts of a poet and thinker whose own world view saw beyond the "two cultures" and who

had felt "the confining walls of scientific method in his time" (1957, p. 13).
And because his full disclosure is inextricably intertwined with his own
attempt to write both nakedly honest autobiography and, at the same time,
a kind of philosophical anthropology, his work provides us with considerably more than just a candid revelation about the workings of science
like Watson's The Double Helix (1980). It causes us to wonder to what
degree mankind's own realization of itself as a species is mirrored in its
supposedly objective pursuit of scientific knowledge and to ask, moreover,
whether both processes are not reflections of the psychological life of scientists themselves. Because Loren Eiseley never separated these processes
within his own mind into water-tight compartments, they flow together
in his work, providing thereby a pure specimen in which to study their
interrelationship.

THE TWO CULTURES

"It is very seldom," the fantasy writer Lord Dunsany once observed,
"that the same man knows much of science, and about the things that were
known before science ever came" (Eiseley, 1969, p. 191). Eiseley was one
such man, a gifted writer who blended imagination, memory, an acute
sense of the miraculous, keen perception, and profound scientific specula-
tion into a single "Orphic voice," as Elizabeth Sewell (1960) has called it."
He paid no attention to the claim of a fellow scientific historian that the
literary naturalist is obsolete.

Eiseley possessed a faith in the unity of things which permitted
him to see, beyond the increasing specialization of his age, that (in the
words of R. Buckminster Fuller) "nature does not have/Separate de-
partments of/Mathematics, physics/Chemistry, biology,/History and lan-
guages,/Which would require/Department head meetings/To decide what
to do/Whenever a boy threw/A stone in the water/With the complex of
consequences/Crossing all departmental lines" (1973, p. 191). Yet his colleagues in the sciences repeatedly attacked him for his open-ended sense of
wonder, which they took to be his "mysticism" and suspected, with some
justification, of being religious in origin, demanding on one occasion, in
words which, Eiseley (1971) explained, sounded "for all the world like a hu-
morless request for the self-accusations so popular in Communist lands . . .
that he "explain" himself (p. 214). Such incidents brought Eiseley to con-
clude that modern science has become a vehicle for the human mind which
has lost all respect for "another world of pure reverie that is of at least equal
importance to the human soul" p. 214), the world his imagination opened
onto.

Not surprisingly, Eiseley's understanding of the connectedness of art and science made him an outspoken critic of the dichotomy of the "two cultures." In an essay specifically addressed to Snow's (1959) conception, for example, he noted that "today's secular disruption between the creative aspect of art and that of science is a barbarism that would have brought lifted eyebrows in a Cro-Magnon cave" (1978, p. 271), and as a writer with the credentials to be accepted in both camps, he exemplified, like other great humanist scientists such as Polanyi and Bronowski, a stereoscopic way of thought which surmounts the illusory division.

Eiseley came to think of himself as a kind of trickster figure, ridiculing the pretensions of science in much the same way that native American "sacred clowns" deride the presumed sanctity of tribal holy men as they perform their rituals. Throughout human history, Eiseley knew, mankind's greatest accomplishments had, until the present age, always been accompanied by "dark shadows"—what the Greek mind called "Nemesis"—which hinted that such triumphs might soon meet with devastation. But with the tremendous upsurge of knowledge introduced by the scientific revolution and the subsequent development of an advanced technology, the "dark shadows" "passed out of all human semblance; no societal ritual safely contained their posturings..." (1969, p. 82). Thus modern science now stands in need of a trickster who would call into question the sanctity and unassailability of science and seek to rein in its longing. Eiseley would certainly have applauded Polanyi's (1968) professed desire to assume a role in relation to science's accomplishments like that of the innocent boy in "The Emperor's New Clothes," pointing an accusing finger at an institution that pretends to be something that, as a human product, it cannot be: objective. Eiseley never forgot that behind the "concealing drapery" of science there always lurks "the swirling vapor of an untamed void whose vassals we are—we who fancy ourselves as the priesthood of powers safely contained and to be exhibited as evidence of our own usurping godhood" (1969, p. 20).

For such attitudes Eiseley had nothing but disdain. He was, for example, disgusted with a United States Senator's announcement (following the moon landing) that men had become "the masters of the universe" (1970, p. 32). He wondered too about the sanity of a prominent scientist who once speculated about what the next ten billion years would offer the species, as if it were a fixed and immutable final product of evolution (1957, pp. 56–57). And he stood amazed at the pomposity of an unnamed turn-of-the-century scientist's proclamation that all generations previous to his own (which had not lived to see Freud, Einstein, or modern genetics) had lived and died in illusion (1975b, p. 5). In contrast to these outrageous instances of species egotism, he quoted with approval von Bertalanffy's insistence that "to grasp in detail ... the physico-chemical organization of the simplest cell is far beyond our capacity" (Eiseley, 1957, p. 206), and he would, I think, have applauded as the highest wisdom Bateson's (1979) definitive assertion that "we shall never be able to claim final knowledge of anything whatsoever" (1979, p. 13). Although he would probably have agreed with Bronowski's contention (1973) that with the scientific revolution human beings committed themselves irreversibly to what amounts to a whole new phase in the evolution of life—and not merely to a cultural innovation—Eiseley insisted again and again that science could never dispense with, nor provide the solutions for the most basic yearnings of our inner life, nor fulfill his almost biological need for an experience of the "holy."

A colleague of Eiseley's (by his own account) once described him as the man who comes "in with furs to warm himself at the stove, but not to stay" (1975a, p. 127). For Eiseley, the scientist was engaged in a walkabout, as the Australian Bushmen call it, a vision quest in search of an understanding of the natural world which would be at the same time an understanding of himself. The wisdom the scientist thus acquired made him, in the end, more than a naturalist: for as he "came to know/a nature still/as time is still/beyond the reach of man" (1972, p. 22), Eiseley became, if you will, a "preternaturalist."

Eiseley (1969) once noted that Circe's admonition to Odysseus in the Odyssey that "magic cannot touch you" (p. 24) was, in fact an initial recognition of the growing scientific mind that would eventually result in twentieth century reductionism, and he strove at all cost never to lose the touch of magic upon himself and his art. Eiseley had little taste for materialist or structuralist explanations in anthropology, sensing in them only signs of disenchantment: "Do not believe those serious-minded men who tell us that writing began with economics and the ordering of jars of oil," he once warned; "Man is, in reality, an oracular animal" (1969, p. 144). He excoriated "men who are willing to pursue evolutionary changes in solitary molar teeth, but never the evolution of ideas" (1975a, p. 195), believing that even scholarship can be the means of revelation for a mind on a vision quest into knowledge. (Eiseley's own brilliant use of his sources, both literary and scientific, lends great credence to the paradoxical assertion of Julius von Sachs—a distinguished botanist—that "all originality comes from reading" [Eiseley, 1975a, p. 187]).

Carlisle (1974) argued that, though his central insights were "extensions of science," Eiseley succeeded in giving "modern biology and anthropology a new idiom" largely because of his ability to interiorize scientific theory (especially the theory of evolution) so that "it functions as a major structure for perceiving and comprehending experience" (pp. 356, 358–59).

Thus the voice of Loren Eiseley, Carlisle explains, "speaks from an inner sky—that vast void within, where science, imagination, and feeling fuse into a vision of existence at once both personal and scientific" (pp. 361). No doubt Carlisle was correct in his estimation; he precisely pinpointed the distinctive source of Eiseley's genius. He only hinted, however, that this process may be inseparable from a personal walkabout which came to take on an archetypal significance, inseparable for Eiseley from "the immense journey"—the odyssey of our species.

Eiseley, after all, envisioned his own work as a gift to his species, a gift of what might be called, after the sociobiologist Richard Dawkins (1976), "memes"—units of cultural transmission, mental replicators (1976, 202–15). Because Eiseley (1969) hoped to create out of a rich inner world an offering to be strewn "like blue plums in some gesture of love toward the universe all outward on a mat of leaves" (p. 232), and in so doing to enhance the species' own faith in the journey it may yet have to run, his writings are filled with questioning about his own possible legacy as a pilot of human longing. He understood from his own experience the mysterious power of books in shaping the course of lives. The most influential book in his own life, he claimed, was The Home Aquarium: How to Care for It, written by a man from New Jersey named Eugene Smith—a book that first inspired Eiseley's interest in the natural world and hence his dual career as a writer and scientist. Looking back in old age on the phenomenal importance of such a book in his life, he pondered the strange effects that books can work over both time and distance: "Did Eugene Smith of Hoboken think his book would have a lifelong impact on a boy in a small Nebraska town? I do not think so" (1975a, p. 170). Such thinking led him to wonder often what the influence of his own books might be in the lives of other human beings without his knowing. Like Bacon, Eiseley seemed to think of his own works as "boats with precious cargoes launched on the great sea of time" (1973, p. 60), and it is impossible not to see his own secret hopes revealed in his suggestion that "like a mutation, an idea may be recorded in the wrong time, to lie latent like a recessive gene and spring once more to life in an auspicious era" (1969, p. 60).

Although childless himself and thus unable to perpetuate his own bio-logical legacy genetically, Eiseley nevertheless shared the dream of all great minds: that his ideas, his insights, his poetry would at least survive him, that his memes would continue to make his presence felt within human history, thus granting him some measure of immortality.

Unlike a scientist, a poet, Bachelard (1958) once remarked, "If he looks through a microscope or a telescope . . . always sees the same thing" (p. 172). He sees always, that is, his own subjectivity, his own self-discovery. Whether he looked into space or into time, Loren Eiseley saw always distance, but he longed for, and eventually discovered, an end to its pursuit. He would not, I think, have agreed with Louis Thomas' (1979) suggestion that it is the poets who will lead us "across the longer stretch of the future," taking over after the scientific mind has completed the exploration of the "near distance" (p. 87–88). Fond of Thomas Love Peacock's assertion that "a poet in our times is a semi-barbarian in a civilized community" whose "march of . . . intellect is like that of crab, backward" (Eiseley, 1970, p. 123), he remained convinced, both temperamentally and philosophically, that "the soul in its creative expression is genuinely not a traveler, that the great writer is peculiarly a product of his native environment" (p. 124). Though he may be the singer of the distance, the caller of the species' journey into the vastness of time, the song, if we could but hear it right, speaks forever of homecoming.

NOBODY COMES HOME TO NOTHINGNESS

Not surprisingly for a man who thought of the pursuit of knowledge as a vision quest, Eiseley was intuitively fascinated with the story of the Odyssey, both with Homer's original version and later recreations of it by Dante, Celli, Tennyson, Pascoli, and Kazantzakis. His books are studded with allusions to these poems: from "The Ghost Continent" in The Unexpected Universe (1969), an extended comparison of the immense journey of the species as revealed by Darwin and Homer's epic, to All the Strange Hours (1975a), where the epigraph for Part One is a line from The Odyssey: "There is nothing worse for mortal men than wandering." His own life in science, in fact, seemed to him "transformed inwardly into something that was whispered to Odysseus long ago" (1969, p. 3) and his own autobiography Odyssean in origin:

> I have penetrated as far as I could dare among rain-dimmed crags and seascapes. But there is more, assuredly there is still more, as Circe tried to tell Odysseus when she warned that death would come to him from the sea. She meant, I think now, the upwelling of that inner tide which engulfs each traveler.
> I have listened belatedly to the warning of the great enchantress. I have cast, while there was yet time, my own oracles on the sun-washed deck. My attempt to read the results contains elements of autobiography. I set it down just as the surge begins to lift, towering and relentless against the reefs of age (1969, p. 25).

"That inner tide" returns at a pivotal moment in All the Strange Hours (1975a) in which the end of his and the species' Odyssey, his death and humankind's death, finally become clear to him, finally become one. But as the above passage's metaphoric richness makes apparent, Eiseley's art/science should be read as an attempt to "read the results," and thus comprehend the meaning, in autobiographical fashion, of Circe's admonition—to interpret oracularly the telos of his Odyssey. (Similarly, Eiseley writes in his Foreword to The Night Country that his books are "the annals of a long and uncompleted running," written "lest the end come on me unawares as it does upon all fugitives" [1971, p. xi]).

It is not too much to say that the Odyssey was the controlling metaphor for Eiseley's own life and for his understanding of human longing as well. James Joyce read twenty four hours in the lives of Leopold and Molly Bloom, Stephen Dedalus and Dublin, as a reenactment in modern dress of the epic's basic morphology; Loren Eiseley saw not just his own life but mankind's as versions of the Odyssey's mythic tale of a voyage out and back. A myth, Levi-Strauss has taught us to see, consists of all of its versions. Eiseley's work, I would like to suggest, may be read an evolutionary interpretation of the Odyssey myth, an interpretation in which both the human mind and Eiseley himself function as dual heroes. Eiseley read the story of the Odyssey as an allegory of the human journey in search of a true spiritual home, guided by a homing instinct; to him its was but a variant of the story of the Prodigal Son. Both are evolutionary tales. But in a post-Darwinian world, such a home to him could be only earthly, not transcendent; it had to be attainable within what Darwin—at the end of The Origin of Species—called the "tangled bank" of evolution, or not at all.

In an illuminating essay, "The Body and the Earth" the poet Wendell Berry (1977) suggested that the Odyssey's significance for us today is to be found in its celebration of essentially ecological values: in its profound understanding of "marriage and household and the earth" (p. 124). A writer who has long criticized the unearthly longing of humankind and celebrated the holiness of place, Berry finds inspiration in its hero's explicit loyalty to a home: "Odysseus' far-wandering through the wilderness of the sea," he reminds us, "is not merely the return of a husband; it is a journey home. And a great deal of the power as well as the moral complexity of The Odyssey rises out of the richness of its sense of home" (p. 125). Indeed, Odysseus' "geographical and moral" journey, Berry suggests, can be "graphed as a series of diminishing circles centered on one of the posts of the marriage bed. Odysseus makes his way from the periphery toward that center" (p. 125). He praises the commitment to placedness implicit in the famous "secret sign"—a marriage bed made from a rooted tree—by which Penelope tests and then recognizes her husband's authenticity. He asks us to recall that Odysseus had embarked on the final leg of his journey home, despite the temptation to remain immortal in the arms of Kalypso, by announcing his desire for his wife in these words:

> My quiet Penelope—how well I know—
> would seem a shade before your majesty,
> death and old age being unknown to you,
> while she must die. Yet, it is true, each
> day I long for home (Berry, 1977, p. 125).

And when, after Odysseus refuses to accept Penelope's order to move their bed outside the bedroom—a violation of a pledge they had made to each other never to do—thereby identifying himself as her true husband after twenty years apart, he finds himself again in her arms. Berry reminds us that Homer compared the reunion to the values of earth:

> Now from his heart into his eyes the ache
> of longing mounted, and he wept at last,
> his dear wife, clear and faithful in his arms, longed for
> as the sunwarmed earth is longed for by a swimmer
> spent in rough water where his ship went down... (p. 127).

As an anti-Iliad, The Odyssey's great theme, Berry wrote, is the value that home assumes for its hero.

Like Berry, Eiseley too admired Homer's telling of the tale because it seemed to him, we might say, a story of faith in the distance and the end of distance. And yet it was not Homer's Odyssey with which he most strongly identified. Giovanni Pascoli's "Ultimo Viaggio," a 1904 reworking of the story's materials, seems to have captivated his imagination most. Pascoli, like Dante, Tennyson, and Kazantzakis, imagined Odysseus, in keeping with the modern, Faustian temperament, becoming restless upon his return home and embarking on yet another—his last—voyage abandoning home again for the open sea. Eiseley (1969) pointed out that Odysseus' return to Ithaca, his homeward goal, was in a sense an anticlimax—that the magical spell wrought by Circe would follow the hero into the prosaic world. But Pascoli's theme is quite different from that of a Kazantzakis, who likewise imagined Odysseus returning to the sea, aspiring to become a world-conquering explorer, or a Tennyson, whose Ulysses dedicated himself forever to be "strong in will,/To strive, to seek, to find, and not to yield," who desires "To follow knowledge like a sinking star,/Beyond the utmost bound of human thought." Pascoli, on the other hand (Eiseley, 1969):

> picks up the Odyssean tale when Odysseus, grown old and restless, drawn on by migratory birds, sets forth to retrace his magical journey, the journey of all men down the pathway of their youth, the road beyond retracing. Circe's isle lies at last before the wanderer

in the plain colors of reality. Circe and whatever she represents have vanished. Much as Darwin might have viewed the Galapagos in old age, Odysseus passes the scenes of the marvelous voyage with all the obstacles reduced to trifles. The nostalgia of space, which is what the Greeks meant by nostalgia, that is, the hunger for home, is transmuted by Pascoli into the hunger for lost time, for the forever vanished days. The Sirens no longer sing, but Pascoli's Odysseus, having read his inward journey, understands them. Knowledge without sympathetic perception is barren. Odysseus in his death is carried by the waves to Calypso, who hides him in her hair. "Nobody" has come home to Nothingness (p. 22).

Eiseley concluded that it was thus Pascoli's great insight "to visualize an end in which the trivial and magicless themselves are transmuted by human wisdom into a timeless dimension having its own enchanted reality" (p. 22).

Loren Eiseley attained in the end a similar wisdom. In his own Odyssey as a writer he, too, returned home—though from a vision quest not a war—and he, too, sought to retrace his steps only to discover finally that his pursuit of distance and his archaeological obsession with time had come to seem an illusion, his great adventure had become indistinguishable from the plain colors of reality. In the end, he too came home to Nothingness. So, too, Eiseley had come to believe, must the species come home, "maturing to finiteness," "dying" into what the earth requires of it.

ROOTED IN THE ABSENCE OF PLACE

When Loren Eiseley died in the summer of 1977, he left the handwritten draft of his last poem, "Beware My Successor" in a drawer of his desk in his office on the University of Pennsylvania campus. The poem (printed in Eiseley, 1979, pp. 97–98) is, as the title suggests, a warning, a curse, for the next individual who might occupy Eiseley's office. He began the poem—which amounts to his last will and testament as a writer—by describing various trees that have fascinated both mankind and him, securing a place in mythology and folklore: the mandragora—a legendary man-eating tree, the hemlock—noted for its poison, yews, oaks, and others. These trees, Eiseley explained, occupied his mind because they have their say through his poetic voice; and what they announce is nothing less than his own imminent end as a human being:

> It is time for you to be gone, your rocks with you,
> your ugly keepsakes of shells, your ancient weapons,
> wood from the dinosaur-age beds,

the rings still showing.
They will say,
Get it out of the way, expendable, the world moves,
old man,
your space is needed (1979, p. 97).

Eiseley agreed with these injunctions, however cruel they may sound, admitting that he would "like to nourish/the man-devouring trees back of my chair or leave the hemlock in my coffee cup." Because he had within him "furies.../that only oak could contain," he welcomed the prospect he envisioned, thanks to the trees' bidding, of being "locked in, with this office as my tomb,/with the bones, the weapons, and the wood." He wanted the end they promised him, longed for a "burial that/recognizes man's true nature," a burial fitting for a man who has "slept beneath redwoods" and whose very "thoughts are gnarled as the redwoods' trunks." In death, he wanted the office he had long inhabited sealed off and "vine leaves to veil my eye sockets,/their giant ropes sustain/me upright in my chair" (1979, pp. 97–98). He ended the poem (and his own career as a writer) with a final admonition:

Beware, my successor;
you have violated
the rites accorded a Druid seer from the sacred groves.
Henceforth I shall linger about here (p. 98).

It is impossible to imagine more appropriate last words or a more fitting summing-up of Eiseley's personal Odyssey, for like T. S. Eliot's "Little Gidding" (1943) they proclaimed in fact that "What we call the beginning is often the end/And to make an end is to make a beginning./The end is where we start from" (p. 58).

The man who makes a vow in childhood, Eiseley noted (quoting Chesterton) in All the Strange Hours (1975a, "makes an appointment with himself at some distant time or place" (p. 166). Eiseley's first vow, he told us, was to read, and his reading, of course, changed him irrevocably. But he made other vows as well, other childhood commitments. Eiseley (1970) recounted how in 1910 he watched Haley's Comet pass overhead while "held in [his] father's arms under the cottonwoods of a cold and leafless spring to see the hurtling emissary of the void." He recalled—in one of his earliest and most cherished memories—how his father had explained to him that the comet would come again only after his death, in his son's old age, and that it would be necessary for the young Eiseley to "live to see it" in his stead. Eiseley acquiesced to his father's expressed wish, "out of love for a sad man who clung to me as I to him" (Eiseley, 1970, pp. 7–8). Eiseley did not, however, live to keep his appointment with the comet.

Unlike Mark Twain, whose birth and death were marked by Haley's appearances, Eiseley died years before he could again witness the comet. But he remained faithful to another childhood commitment, also made with his father.

In "The Brown Wasps" in The Night Country (1971) Eiseley recalled how, over sixty years earlier when he was about six years old, he had helped his father plant a cottonwood sapling near his boyhood home in Nebraska. The tree, like the promise to see Haley's comet, was in reality an appointment with the future. For as a child, he explained, he had watered it faithfully—even on the day, years later after his father's death, when he moved away from his original home. Although all those who were "supposed to wait and grow old under [the tree's] shade" either "died or moved away" from the small Nebraska town in which it grew, Eiseley, at least, managed to return in old age, during a time of "long inward struggle," to witness again first hand the tree he had planted and cared for as a young boy (pp. 227–36).

During his sixty years away, Eiseley's prodigal mind never forgot the tree; for it had, he observed, "for some intangible reason" (1971, p. 234) taken root in his mind. It was under its branches that he sheltered; it was from this tree that his memories led away into the world. It had become, he admitted, "part of my orientation in the universe," something without which he could not exist. For during his lifetime it had been "growing in my mind, a huge tree that somehow stood for my father and the love I bore him," and as a symbol, as well, for the "attachment of the spirit to a grouping of events in time" (p. 235). It was a natural emblem of his own individuation, his own immense journey from the timeless world of his childhood—in which he had nestled among migrating birds in a hedgerow—into his time-obsessed maturity.

But having returned in time to the place where the "real" tree grew, Eiseley discovered to his alarm that it was gone, that his life has been passed "in the shade of a non-existent tree." Disillusioned, his life seemed to him momentarily without meaning; he longed only to flee the scene of this outrage to his dignity. But as he tried to escape, a small boy on a tricycle followed him, quite curious about the stranger who wandered about his neighborhood. In despair, disoriented without the tree which had for so long centered him in the world and in time, Eiseley nostalgically recalled his father's words at the time of the tree's first planting: "We'll plant a tree here, son, and we're not going to move any more. And when you're an old, old man you can sit under it and think how we planted it here, you and me together."

With this memory, the anguish of Eiseley's own immense journey has reached its nadir; for, in his prodigal pursuit of the distance in time as well as space, he had been completely unfaithful to his father's fervent hope for him. His vow to his father has been broken: his appointment with his future self had brought him only grief. And yet, as his steps quickened the boy on the tricycle called out to the departing stranger a question: "Do you live here mister?" To answer the question Eiseley took "a firm grip on airy nothing—to be precise, on the bole of a great tree," and responds firmly, "I do." For he realized that in his imagination he had come home, an easy accomplishment. His imagination, at least, had never left home. Having been formed there, its own centripetal force inclined it always toward its home, its center.

Like Yeats in "Among School Children," Eiseley had discovered that only the symbol of a tree can answer man's perpetual questions about illusion and reality, life and death, innocence and maturity, the near and the far. In a tree it is impossible to distinguish "the dancer from the dance," or being from becoming, and all opposites become united—even nearness and distance. In answer to the child's question—and is not the child an avatar of Eiseley's own young tree-planting self?—Eiseley's reply of "I do" was truly a marriage vow. Because he understood–like Pascoli's Odysseus— that his journey away from home, and all the trials of that journey, had all been illusory, just as the tree itself had been. He wedded his own roots with his own growth, his strangeness with his commonality, his prodigality with his point of departure. In the irony of such an insight his eyes opened to a world "in which the trivial and magicless themselves are transmuted by human wisdom into a timeless dimension having its own enchanted reality." Nobody comes home to nothingness.

Mankind's uniqueness, Bronowski (1973) once observed, comes from the fact that we, alone among all living creatures, have experiences that never happen, except in our imaginations, experiences that are every bit as important as those that do happen. Though "non-existent," Eiseley's tree, in his imagination, shaped his entire life's journey. The truly "concrete," Whitehead (1925) explains in Science and the Modern World, is "that which has grown together" (p. 174). Though imaginary, nothing in Eiseley's odyssey had served more powerfully as a concrete force in shaping his experience than the tree. Like the always centered point of Donne's famous compass in "A Valediction Forbidding Mourning," it had grounded his journey into time and space, centering it always in its place and time of origin. Eiseley's odyssey, like the original one, had been a journey "from the periphery toward [a] center," a center that was, in fact, a tree. His journey had, in fact, been the tree's real growth; and his reply to the boy's question was true, but a truth Eiseley had only just discovered.

As Howard Gruber (1978) has taught us to see, creative work is often guided by an "image of wide scope": "a schema capable of assimilating to

itself a wide range of perceptions, actions, ideas." Such an image, Gruber
(1981) showed, guided Darwin's discovery of evolution by natural selection and may very well help to shape creative advances in a number of
fields. The particular importance of any given "image of wide scope"—as
Gruber (1978) noted—"depends in part on the metaphoric structure peculiar to the given image, in part on the intensity of the emotion which has
been invested in it, that is, its value to the person." Clearly, Eiseley's imaginary tree was such an image, one in which he placed tremendous value.
It showed him how to be, in Simone Weil's phrase, "rooted in the absence
of place" (1977, p. 356) But like every image in his work, every event in his
Odyssey, its meaning was not solely ontogenetic.

Of his two childhood appointments Eiseley kept only one. The desire
to follow the comet's inter-galactic journey sprang, Eiseley seemed to sense,
from the same Faustian longing that had made man a world-eater and,
inevitably, a spore-bearer as well, and since he tried to disavow himself
from these tendencies in order to become once again a mere creature within
the world order, it seems fitting that he failed to keep his rendezvous with
the comet and answered only the tree's summons. It was his faithfulness to
its earthly ways, after all, that brought him to proclaim himself in his last
poem a "Druid seer" and enabled him to hear and understand the trees'
"plans" for him at his life's close; for only a tree—an "oak's strength"—
could in the end "contain his furies" (1979, p. 98).

But Eiseley sensed that even these two seemingly disparate sides of
himself—and of the species—were not irreconcilable. The human project,
and our longing for space, must, he believed, end as his own had done, in
a turning homeward:

> The task is admittedly gigantic, but even Haley's flaming star has
> rounded on its track, a pinpoint of light in the uttermost void. Man
> like the comet, is both bound and free. Throughout the human genera-
> tions the star has always turned homeward. *Nor do man's inner journeys
> differ from that far-flung elliptic* (1970, pp. 155–56).

Our era, Eiseley observed, had already witnessed the perfect symbol of
such a "turning": the Apollo 13 mission crew's decision to risk a hazardous
re-entry into the earth's atmosphere rather than remain marooned in lunar
orbit. To Eiseley, their motivation seemed clear and revealing:

> A love for earth, almost forgotten in man's roving mind, had momen-
> tarily reasserted its mastery, a love for the green meadows we have so
> long taken for granted and desecrated to our cost. Man was born and
> took shape among earth's leafy shadows. The most poignant thing the
> astronauts had revealed in their extremity was the nostalgic call still
> faintly ringing on the winds from the sunflower forest (1970, p. 156).

The life of the species, then, the Odyssey of the species through time has transpired, like the maturation of Eiseley himself, within the shadow of a "non-existent tree." Born amidst "earth's leafy shadows," having descended from the trees to become world conquerors, the prodigal, too, seems to have left its home in the natural world far behind him in the course of his immense journey. But the natural world still calls out to him to return, as if he had a future appointment with it that he has forgotten. The human mind is tethered to the Earth, inextricably under the sway of a geologic, just as Eiseley's mind was tethered to his tree, and evolution is the tether, and the symbol of the tethering is a tree:

> We today know the results of Darwin's endeavors—the knitting together of the vast web of life until it is seen like the legendary tree of Igdrasil, reaching endlessly up through the dead geological strata with living and relevant branches still glowing in the sun (1969, p. 133).

In Norse mythology, Igdrasil, the world tree, a mythic "image of wide scope," unites within its roots and branches all things: heaven, earth, and the underworld. So, too, Igdrasil in a sense is meant: for it has only been through the human mind that the "web of life" becomes known—becomes conscious of itself. Thus Eiseley the "druid seer" recognized that as an individual he was an Igdrasil as well:

> I too am aware of the trunk that stretches loathsomely back of me along the floor. I too am a many-visaged thing that has climbed upward out of the dark of endless leaf falls, and has slunk, furred, through the glitter of blue glacial nights. I, the professor trembling absurdly on the platform with my book and spectacles, am the single philosophical animal. I am the unfolding worm, and mud fish, the weird tree of Igdrasil shaping itself endlessly out of darkness toward the light (1975b, p. 168).

REFERENCES

Bachelard, G. (1958). *The poetics of space*. Trans. Maria Jolas. Boston: Beacon Press.
Bateson, G. (1979). *Mind and nature: a necessary unity*. New York: E. P. Dutton.
Berry, W. (1984). *Collected poems*. San Francisco: North Point Press.
Berry, W. (1977). *The unsettling of America: culture and agriculture*. New York: Avon Books.
Bronowski, J. (1973). *The ascent of man*. Boston: Little, Brown.
Carlisle, E.F. (1983). *Loren Eiseley: The development of a writer*. Urbana: University of Illinois Press.
Carlisle, E.F. (1974). The heretical science of Loren Eiseley. *The Centennial Review*. 18, 354–77.
Dawkins, R. (1976). *The selfish gene*. New York: Oxford University Press.
Eiseley, L. (1979). *All the night wings*. New York: Times Books.
Eseley, L. (1975b). *The firmament of time*. New York: Atheneum.
Eiseley, L. (1975a). *All the strange hours: An excavation of a life*. New York: Charles Scribner.

Eiseley, L. (1973). *The man who saw through time*. New York: Scribner.

Eiseley, L. (1972). *Notes of an alchemist*. New York: Scribner.

Eiseley, L. (1971). *The night country*. New York: Scribner.

Eiseley. (1970). *The invisible pyramid*. New York: Scribner.

Eiseley, L. (1969). *The unexpected universe*. New York: Harcourt, Brace Jovanovich.

Eiseley, L. (1957). *The immense journey*. New York: Vintage.

Eliot, T.S. (1943). *Four quartets*. New York: Harcourt, Brace and World.

Fuller, R.B. (1973). *Intuition*. Garden City: Doubleday.

Gruber, H.E (1981). *Darwin on man: A psychological study of scientific creativity*. Chicago: University of Chicago Press.

Gruber, H.E. (1978). Darwin's "Tree of Nature" and other images of wide scope. In Judith N. Wechsler (Ed.), *On aesthetics in nature*, pp.121–40. Cambridge: MIT Press.

Hillman, J. (1975). *Re-visioning psychology*. New York: Harper and Row.

Kazantzakis, N. (1958). *The Odyssey: a modern sequel*. Trans. Kimon Friar. New York: Touchstone.

Levi-Strauss, C. (1955). *Tristes tropiques*. Trans. John and Doreen Weightman. New York: Washington Square Press.

Macbeth, N. (1971). *Darwin retried*. New York: Dell.

Polanyi, M. (1968). A conversation With Michael Polanyi. *Psychology Today*, pp. 20, 22–25, 66–67.

Polanyi, M. (1962). *Personal knowledge: Toward a post-critical philosophy*. Chicago: University of Chicago Press.

Rilke, R.M. (1978). *Where silence reigns: Selected prose*. Trans. G. Craig Houston. New York: New Directions.

Sewell, E. (1960). *The orphic voice: Poetry and natural history*. New York: Harper and Row.

Snow, C.P. (1959). *The two cultures and the scientific revolution*. New York: Cambridge University Press.

Thomas, L. (1979). *The medusa and the snail: More notes of a biology watcher*. New York: Bantam.

Watson, J. (1980). The double helix: a personal account of the discovery of the structure of DNA. In Gunther S Stent (Ed.), *Norton Critical Edition*. New York: W.W. Norton.

Weil, S. (1977). *A Simone Weil Reader*. George A. Panichas (Ed.), New York: McKay.

Whitehead, A.N. (1925). *Science and the modern world*. New York: Free Press.

Wilson, E.O. (1978). *On human nature*. Cambridge: Harvard University Press.

2

IRONY AND CONFLICT
LESSONS FROM GEORGE BERNARD SHAW'S WARTIME JOURNEY

Michael Hanchett Hanson

World War I was both tragic and transforming for George Bernard Shaw. Like Europe as a whole, Shaw confronted the limits of his own views and strategies during the Great War. The distinctive Shavian voice that had changed the face of socialism in Britain in the 1880s; the voice that helped build the prestige of the Fabian Society, and, thereby, laid the foundation for the British Labor Party; the voice that had conveyed Shaw's political perspectives through theater, journalism, debates and lectures; the voice that had made him famous worldwide—the Shavian irreverent and ironic confrontation of his audience seemed to fail when Shaw confronted Europe at war.

The problem was not the quality of insight. Many of Shaw's views on the war were uncannily prescient. In the Fall of 1914 he foresaw a long, bloody war. He predicted a second war if the peace terms were vindictive. He predicted a longer-term conflict between Russia and the West. He emphasized the essential role of the United States for ultimate victory, and he prescribed a Western European mutual defense pact that included Germany as the key to enduring European peace. In his 1914 essay, *Common Sense about the War* (1914/1931, hereafter, *Common Sense*), Shaw laid out these insights as a coherent set of warnings about the present and vision for the future. Not all of his ideas were entirely new. Some, like the European mutual defense pact, he had advocated before the war (Shaw,

1913/1931). Laying out such a vision at that particular moment in history, however, was extraordinary—and that *was* part of the problem.

The world was not receptive to such extraordinary ideas. Even though *Common Sense* was read by a wide and influential audience, including U.S. President Wilson (Weintraub, 1971), Shaw had little direct influence on his government's policies during the conflict. Many Britons were outraged by Shaw's positions. Even some of his oldest and closest friends would distance themselves from him over the war.

In the end, Shaw's wartime journey would be extraordinary for both its breadth of ideas and depth of moral conviction. *Common Sense*, and Shaw's subsequent writing during the war, reflected years of thinking about the impact of international relations on the goals of social justice to which Shaw devoted his life. Staying true to those convictions in the face of overwhelming public opposition was courageous. Maintaining his good humor in the face of public and personal attacks demonstrated a commitment to ending the war that went far beyond Shaw's concern for his own reputation.

In this chapter, I examine how ironic thinking contributed to Shaw's initial point of view and to changes in his perspective on the war. This is a story of moral passion from beginning to end. It is also a story of growth. Finally and inescapably, it is an examination of what Shaw's irony may mean to us, at the beginning of the 21st century.

THE BIOGRAPHICAL JOURNEY

In August, 1914, Bernard Shaw was 58 years old. He was at the height of his career as a playwright and Fabian activist. In the 38 years since he arrived in London from Dublin, Shaw had transformed himself from an impoverished, shy, awkward, uneducated young man into one of the most famous and outspoken men in the world.

From "Corno di Bassetto" to Quintus Fabius Maximus

When Shaw first came to London, he spent much of his time at the British Museum Library, educating himself on topics ranging from philosophy to economics to opera to social etiquette. His initial success as an author was in journalism, writing art, music and theater criticism. In his music reviews Shaw literally made a name for himself as "Corno di Bassetto" and as "GBS." And, from the beginning, his writing was full of irony and confrontation. For example, in a column on a performance of Handel's *Messiah*, Shaw "defended" the natural English voice against the criticism of musical slowness by noting that "the natural fault of the English when they are singing with genuine feelings is not slowness, but rowdiness, as the neighbors of the Salvation Army know" (Shaw, 1891/1955, p. 250). This was not the usual music review. Shaw's lively style helped make his columns accessible and fun. At the same time, his expertise and high standards were obvious. In the estimation of W. H. Auden, Shaw "was probably the best music critic who ever lived" (1942/1953, p. 156).

During his early years in London Shaw also became a socialist. In the 1880s he discovered and virtually took over the Fabian Society, a disorganized group of socialists named after the Roman general, Quintus Fabius Maxiumus. The original Fabius purportedly defeated Hannibal by patiently waiting out his enemy until the right moment for battle, and throughout their history the Fabians have been committed to promoting socialist ideals by picking the right political battles, rather than supporting revolution. Shortly after joining the Fabians, Shaw wrote a *Manifesto* for the group. The irreverent and entertaining Shavian voice was as new to socialism as it had been to art criticism, and Shaw helped attract some of the leading socialist minds to the Fabians. Under the guidance primarily of Shaw and Sidney and Beatrice Webb, the group grew in number and reputation. In 1900 the Fabians joined with Trade Unions to form the Labor Party. Then, in 1913 the Fabians launched a newspaper, the *New Statesman*, for which Shaw was one of the major financial underwriters. All of these efforts have had enduring impact. At the beginning of the 21st century, the Fabian Society, the *New Statesman* and the Labor Party remain major forces in British political life.

From "chocolate cream soldiers" to "not bloody likely"

In spite of these political accomplishments, today, Shaw is probably best known for his plays. He began writing plays in the 1890s as a creative enterprise, as a way to make money and as a vehicle for his socialist ideals. From the beginning, his plays were controversial. Shaw could not find a producer for his second play, *The Philanderer* (1898/1980c), and his third play, *Mrs. Warren's Profession* (1898/1980a), was banned by the censors. Even *Pygmalion* (1916/1973), which opened in 1914 caused an uproar with the line "not bloody likely" (p. 55) Of course, as Shaw had learned early, controversy can be an element of success, and *Pygmalion* was a box-office hit that both expanded Shaw's fame and helped ensure his financial security.

The socialist Fabians focused primarily on reforming domestic, social and economic issues in Great Britain, and Shaw's plays were his special versions of the comedy of manners genre, often literally set in drawing rooms. Surprisingly, then, from early in Shaw's career, war and militarism were important topics in his plays. Indeed, Shaw's first successful play,

Arms and the Man (1894/1960) was about a fictional Balkan war. The play debunks romantic concepts of war and heroism from the opening scene in which a professional soldier, who is more concerned about having chocolates than ammunition, hides in a young lady's room. Shaw went on to write *The Man of Destiny* (1898/1941, about Napoleon), *Caesar and Cleopatra: A History* (1898/1942), and *Captain Brassbound's Conversion: An Adventure* (1899/1941), all of which included themes of militarism or war, and were written before his first major Fabian pamphlet on the subjects, *Fabianism and Empire* (1900). In other words, Shaw began looking at war from the perspective of the theater where, as he noted in the preface to *Heartbreak House* (1919d), "the fights are sham fights, and the slain, rising the moment the curtain has fallen, go comfortably home to supper after washing off their rose-pink wounds" (pp. xli–xlii).[1]

Thus, on the eve of war, Shaw was accustomed to success against great odds, and he had achieved his success through confrontation and controversy. He had a distinctive vision for what the world was and could be, and had devoted both his theatrical and political work to that vision. In particular, he had learned to use his theatrical mind to think about war.

From Common Sense to Heartbreak

When WWI began, Shaw was on vacation in Torquay, a seaside resort on the shore of the English Channel. He immediately cloistered himself at his hotel and began writing about the war. Out of that work came his soon-to-be-infamous 70-page essay, *Common Sense About the War*.

The essay was published as an extensive supplement to the *New Statesman* on November 13, 1914. In it, Shaw took the position that the war was a senseless fight between the German and English aristocrats and militarists in which the ultimate losers would be the general populace of both countries. He recounted in detail the history of demonizing propaganda by both sides, beginning in the 19th century, and the more recent diplomatic history leading to the war. Shaw contended that, now that the war had begun, England and France (with the necessary help of the United States) must win, but the ultimate peace must not be vindictive. He then prescribed the key aspects of a desirable armistice. Throughout, Shaw derided the hypocrisy and self-righteousness of the English in general and the diplomats in particular. He also criticized the duplicity of the Church,

---

[1] Moving between political essays and plays on a topic was not just a way of expressing ideas, but a way of thinking about them. Shavian scholar Martin Meisel (1971/1987) has analyzed the ways Shaw treated subjects in his plays and in his political essays. Meisel found that, up to *Heartbreak House*, Shaw tended to take more extreme positions in the plays.

contending that its ministers were following the war god Mars in the name of the Prince of Peace. In *Common Sense* Shaw attacked almost every conceivable assumption that would justify a vindictive war, allowing only the pragmatic arguments for continuing the fight, now that it had begun. As his biographer, Michael Holroyd (1991), has written, "Shaw's position in *Common Sense about the War* was that of the Irishman who, when asked for directions, replies that he wouldn't start from here" (p. 351).

As previously mentioned, the public reactions to Shaw's position on the war were overwhelmingly negative. H. G. Wells' (1914) attack was especially notable. Wells described Shaw as:

> One of those perpetual children who live in a dream world of make-believe . . . It is almost as if there was no pain in all the world. It is under the inspiration of such delightful dreams that Mr. Shaw now flings himself upon his typewriter and rattles out his broadsides. And nothing will stop him. All through the war we shall have this Shavian accompaniment going on, like an idiot child screaming in a hospital, distorting, discrediting, confusing. . . . He is at present . . . an almost unendurable nuisance (p. 6).

Wells was not alone in publicly attacking Shaw's positions on the war, and there were other consequences. The Dramatists' Club informed Shaw that, due to his views on the war, he would not be invited to further meetings. Previously friendly newspapers refused to print Shaw's work (Ervine, 1956; Weintraub, 1971; Holroyd, 1991). Even Shaw's old friends and Fabian allies, Sidney and Beatrice Webb, distanced themselves from his positions on the war. By 1916—only three years after the founding of the paper—Shaw felt that his policy disagreements with his old friends, the Webbs, left him no choice but to resign from the *New Statesman* Board of Directors.

> In 1918, he wrote to fellow socialist Augustin Hamon: I have no effective influence with the Labor Party. The Fabian Society is represented on it by Sidney Webb . . . I could not impose my views on the Labor Party, nor even place them effectively before it (March 9, 1918, in Laurence, 1985, pp. 536–537).

In spite of the negative reactions, Shaw stuck to his conceptual guns. During the war, he continued to write essays, expanding on the wide range of themes he had addressed in *Common Sense*. Those works included essays about British patriotism, compulsory conscription, military censorship and conscientious objectors, as well as reports from the front. He also wrote four one-act plays on war themes: *O'Flaherty, V.C.* (1919f), *The Inca of Perusalem* (1919e), *Augustus Does His Bit* (1919b) and *Annajanska, the Bolshevik Empress* (1919a).

Shaw's major play about the war, however, was *Heartbreak House* (1919d) which he wrote from 1916–1917 with unusual difficulty for a man accustomed to writing plays *"d'un seul trait"* (letter to Mrs. Patrick Campbell, May 14, 1916, in Dent, 1952, p. 209). As was Shaw's practice, he wrote the preface last (in 1919), in this case waiting until the war was over. The play and the preface are stinging indictments of the European leisure classes before the war, including the class of the Fabian leadership to which he had belonged. The play was actually conceived at a summer country house that Shaw had shared with the Webbs and Leonard and Virginia Woolf during the war (Shaw in Laurence, 1988).

Heartbreak House (1919d) is an allegorical comedy of manners with a surprise ending. Characters, representing different aspects of society, find themselves together in a country house, playing the cat-and-mouse match-making games of the genre, with Shaw's usual cutting social commentary. Without warning to those onstage or in the audience, the zeppelins come at the end of the play. The zeppelins exhilarate all of the people in the house, except two. Those two run for safety and are killed by the bombs. The others in the house remain transfixed and thrilled.

"Sh-sh! Listen: do you hear it now? It's magnificent" (1919d, p. 120), says the mistress of the house, Mrs. Hushabye, about the sound of the zeppelins. Her husband turns on all of the lights in the house so that the zeppelins can see it, and says, "We of this house are only moths flying into the candle" (1919d, p. 120). When the zeppelins have left:, Mrs. Hushabye remarks, "But what a glorious experience. I hope they'll come again tomorrow night" (1919d, p. 122).

In this ending, leisure led to catastrophe: the characters' fate was sealed without them even knowing it was in the balance. Then, like "moths flying into the candle," they embraced their own potential destruction. According to Robert Corrigan (1959), "It is in *Heartbreak House* that Shaw first came to grips without equivocation with those questions that haunted Ibsen, Strindberg, and Chekhov before him. How is one to live in an irrational world?" (p. 2).

THE COGNITIVE JOURNEY

An examination of Shaw's ironic thought during the war is instructive on a number of levels. For those of us interested in creative development and in cognitive semantics, Shaw's case provides an example of how irony can function in creative thinking. This is new territory. Case study research, using the Evolving Systems approach, has focused on the roles of metaphor in creative thinking (e.g., Gruber, 1974/1981, 1978; Osowski, 1989), but not on irony.

The historical context of Shaw's irony is also important. Some of his ironic views may be considered examples of WWI historian Paul Fussell's (1975/2000) thesis: "that there seems to be one dominating form of modern understanding; that it is essentially ironic; and that it originates largely in the application of mind and memory to the events of the Great War" (p. 35). Shaw's thinking at the beginning of WWI also stands in contrast to the sense of regret that has characterized that legacy of irony. Shaw's irony was initially used largely to analyze strategies, see through prejudice, predict outcomes and formulate proposals. Fussell refers to an ironic understanding that comes, in part, from so many of those prejudices being acted out, so many of the predictions being true.

Our own understanding of Shaw's irony is also part of the 20th-century legacy. Much of this study examines Shaw's clearly marked—i.e., overt—irony for which least interpretation is necessary. But, inescapably, this study is also an interpretive link across time, a link in which both Shaw's sense of irony and our own come into play. Indeed, today's concepts of irony are among the defining elements of the journey.

THE CHALLENGE OF IRONY

At the beginning of his influential typology of irony, literary critic D. C. Muecke (1969) wrote:

> Getting to grips with irony seems to have something in common with gathering mist; there is plenty to take hold of if only one could. To attempt a taxonomy of a phenomenon so nebulous that it disappears as one approaches is an even more desperate adventure. Yet if, upon examination, irony becomes less nebulous, as it does, it remains elusively Protean (p. 3).

With quixotic valor Muecke then went on to delineate an extensive and influential typology. Part of his inspiration for taking on that challenge was the expansion of the concept of irony, which grew in breadth and importance over the course of the 20th century.

The Expanding Concept

The opening line of *Common Sense* was overt irony. Shaw began his essay with a quote from Graham Wallas:

> Let a European War break out—the war, perhaps, between the Triple Alliance and the Triple Entente, which so many journalists and politicians in England and Germany contemplate with criminal levity. If the combatants prove to be equally balanced, it may, after the first battles,

smoulder on for thirty years. What will be the population of London,
or Manchester, or Chemnitz, or Bremen, or Milan, at the end of it?
(Wallas, 1914, in Shaw, 1914/1931, p. 19)

Here, the imperative—"Let a European War break out"—is ironic by
any measure. Wallas's words fit the common definition of irony as saying
the opposite of what the writer apparently means. That was a widely held
definition of irony in Shaw's time. The Romantics had advocated a much
broader view of irony during the 19th century, but the old inversion-of-
meaning concept was more common, even among intellectuals. For example, in *Jokes and Their Relation to the Unconscious*, Freud (1905/1960) defined
irony as simply the technique of "representation by the opposite" (p. 86).

By the late 20th century, however, irony had taken on broader meaning,
reviving some 19th-century Romantic concepts with 20th-century twists.
The result has been an array of concepts of irony that have been applied to
literature (e.g., Brooks, 1947; Wilde, 1981; Hutcheon, 1994); historiography
(White, 1973); architecture (Venturi, 1977); philosophy (e.g., de Man, 1979;
Rorty, 1989; Ankersmit, 1996); and Postmodern criticism (e.g., Hutcheon,
1988, 1994; Lemert, 1992).

Shavian criticism represents some of the changes in our concepts of
irony. During his long life Shaw was accused of being a "paradoxer" (Shaw,
1898/1980b), but was rarely labeled an "ironist." Shortly after Shaw's death,
in a collection of criticism about Shaw by some of the leading thinkers of
the first half of the 20th century, irony was not emphasized. For example,
G. K. Chesterton (1909/1953) wrote of Shaw's wit:

> It must be remembered that Shaw emerged as a wit in a sort of sec-
> ondary age of wits; one of those interludes of prematurely old young
> men, which separate the serious epochs of history. Oscar Wilde was
> its god.... One of its notes was an artificial reticence of speech, which
> waited till it could plant the perfect epigram. (p. 28)

In that same publication, W. H. Auden (1942/1953) described what
we think of as Shavian irony as an antidote to logical fallacy: "He cannot,
thank God, be serious for long: the more logical his argument, the more
certain he is to accompany it with a wink" (p. 155).

By the late 20th century, in keeping with general theories of irony,
Weintraub (1966/1970) referred to "the kinds of ironic wit Shaw loved"
(p. 343); Fred Mayne (1967) compared the structure of Shavian drama to
Socratic Irony, and literary critic Harold Bloom (1987) saw Shaw as "a crafty
ironist" (p. 8).

Of course, history is seldom neat. During the war, Shaw himself wrote
that "the war is full of ironies" (letter to Dorothy Mackenzie, March 18,
1918, in Laurence, 1985, p. 546). In other words, in examining Shaw's ironic

thinking about WWI, we are looking at a period in which the concept of irony was on the brink of the rapid expansion that it would undergo during the rest of the century. If Fussell is right about the link of WWI to modern ironic understanding, the war may also have contributed to the expansion of the concept.

The present research applies current ideas about irony to Shaw's descriptions of situations and his use of verbal techniques. Rather than examining the role of irony in creative thought, for much of this research we are examining those definitions of paradox and wit from earlier in the century that are now considered forms of irony. But the changes in our concepts of irony are still important. We will return to this issue when we consider what this research may mean for us, at the beginning of the 21st century.

Irony as Creative Thought

Today's theories tend to define irony along a number of axes. We can think of irony as verbal or situational; as dynamic or structure; as overt or covert; as stance or meaning; as isolated incidents or broad world views. In the initial leg of our own journey we will consider Shaw's thinking in relation to these aspects of irony.

For any consideration of irony, we also have theories from multiple disciplines. There are the long Western traditions of irony in literature, rhetoric and philosophy, going back to ancient Greece, as well as more recent cultural theories and psychological investigations. And, of course, within each discipline there are different approaches. For example, in psychology recent research has examined irony as a figure of thought (Gibbs, 1994); as verbal comprehension (Winner, 1988; Gibbs, 1994; Sperber & Wilson, 1995; Kreuz, 2000); as allusion pretense (Kumon-Nakamura, Glucksberg and Brown, 1995); as event knowledge (Lucariello, 1994); as metarepresentational reasoning (Lucariello & Mindolovich, 1995); as compromise formations (Stringfellow, 1994), and as self-control outcomes (Wegner, 1994).

In this study, we draw from some of the ancient concepts, but, primarily use 20th-century psychological and cultural approaches to irony. This emphasis reflects key aspects of the investigation: the creative thought that went into Shaw's texts and the interpretation of them in the early 20th century as well as today. As background, a few principles, derived from today's concepts of irony, will be helpful.

Principle 1: All Irony is Ultimately Situational
Raymond Gibbs, Jr. (1994) has analyzed irony as a figure of thought and has noted its ultimate situational basis: "Verbal and situational irony,

although mostly distinct, are related in one important way, in that speakers' intentional use of verbal irony reflects their conceptualizations of situations as ironic" (p. 365). In other words, verbal irony is a compressed reference to a situation.

An example of this principle is Shaw's explanation of the meaning of "Junker" in *Common Sense* (1914/1931). Having noted the negative stereotypes of German Junkers as cruel and uncivilized, Shaw suggested that his English audience "resort to a dictionary" (p. 22). The dictionary defined Junkers as country gentlemen. Based on that definition, Shaw pointed out, "Thus we can see that the Junker is by no means peculiar to Prussia. We can claim to produce the article in perfection that may well make Germany despair of ever surpassing us in that line" (1914/1931, p. 22).

He went on to list leaders of the British government who were Junkers. Finally, Shaw remarked that, "of course, the Kaiser is a Junker, though less true-blue than the Crown Prince . . . " (1914/1931, p. 22). Here we confront the difference between overt and covert irony, as well as the importance of knowing the situation in order to appreciate verbal irony. At an overt level, this irony was the same as the overall situation explicitly described—the pot calling the kettle black. The Crown Prince was a Junker like the Kaiser. With more knowledge of the situation, however, the irony holds added punch. The British Royal family was largely of German descent and, indeed, their name was Saxe-Coburg-Gotha. During WWI, to distance themselves from their enemy, the Royal Family would take the name "Windsor" (royal.gov.uk, 2002). The crown prince was not just like a German Junker, he *was* a German Junker. In other words, fully appreciating the verbal irony in the "true-blue" reference, required knowing the situation.

From a psychological perspective, the situational root of irony can be described as deviation from standard event scripts. A script is a learned expectation about the way the world works (Schank & Abelson, 1977). For example, going to a restaurant entails a series of events, a "script". In the restaurant script, behaviors are linked to goals in ways that are learned and contextually appropriate to the culture. Research has shown that people depend on such scripts to give meaning to narratives. In recall, people tend to restore missing parts to a script and to reorder a scrambled script. An occurrence that does not fit the script tends to be ignored or given meaning specifically in its anomalous relation to the script (Bransford, 1979; Ashcraft, 1989).

Historical treatment of WWI can be seen as an example of such cognitive compensation. Witness historian Esmé Wingfield-Stratford's (1968) comments:

> It had been assumed by the experts who planned it, and was taken for granted by the propaganda-drunken masses, that this was going to be

a war of battles and decisions in the old style, over, like the European
ones of the mid-nineteenth century, in a matter of weeks or months.
The military mind, whose nature it is always to think of the present
in terms of the past, had utterly failed to appreciate the revolutionary
change in the nature of warfare ... (p. 384)

In other words, in 1914, Europe had a well-established event script for
war. One of the many aspects of WWI that did not fit the script was the
slow and indecisive trench warfare. Then, just as the psychological theory
would predict, "A vast literature has been produced in the attempt to bring
it [WWI] into line with other wars by highlighting its so-called battles by
such impressive names as Loos, Verdun, the Somme and Passchendaele
... " (Wingfield-Stratford, 1968, p. 386). This misalignment of WWI to the
war script does not strike us as particularly ironic, however. Conceptual
compensation is made, rather than irony highlighted. All script anomalies
are not ironic.

Joan Lucariello (1994) investigated the relationship between situational irony and event scripts. She proposed that situational irony was
a specific kind of script-anomalous event, not simply an unexpected element. To test this hypothesis, Lucariello condensed and revised Muecke's
(1969) literary taxonomy of irony into 7 categories with 27 subcategories
(e.g., *role reversals, self-betrayal, loss/loss recurrence*). She then conducted a
series of experiments to find out whether or not naïve adult subjects could
both reliably produce and classify ironic situations using the taxonomy. She
found they could, and she concluded that ironic situations are related to
nonironic event scripts. But ironic situations are culturally recognized types
of deviations from scripts, with conceptual coherence that distinguishes
them from simple anomalies. In other words, the ironic situation is not just
unexpected. It also fits patterns that we have learned to recognize as ironic.

Principle 2: The Ironic Situation Requires an Alazon
The Western concept of irony originated in ancient Greek theater
where two stock characters were the *eiron* and the *alazon*. The *eiron*, or
ironist, understated her true position as a technique for deflating her natural prey, the *alazon*, or "victim" of the irony, who overstated his position,
abilities, etc. (Aristotle, 1990; Frye, 1957/1990; Muecke, 1969). Irony, thus,
originated as a role. In later usage, the concept expanded to include the
techniques the ironist uses and situations that reflect her perceptions.

Muecke (1969) contended that, even for 20th-century concepts of situational irony, the roles of ironist, victim and observer were still necessary.
But those roles were not always distinct. Often the ironist was abstractly
implied as nature or fate, and the "victim" not even in the room. Two
people alone could comment wryly about "British Junkers" without those

accused ever hearing the comments. The mere fact that particular Britons would not perceive the irony—or are simply *imagined* as not getting it—is enough to fulfill the "victim" requirement. Indeed, "victim" brings with it allusions that do not always fit the *alazon's* role. The bottom line of that role is that the person or group be naïvely unaware of the possibility of the irony (Muecke, 1969). This is a type of conceit that can come from innocence, prejudice or over-confidence in a naïf, a buffoon or a villain.

To make it all a bit more complex, the roles of ironist and *alazon* some-times overlap. Muecke and others (e.g., Frye, 1957/1990; Wilde, 1981) have linked irony to broader world views. In Muecke's typology, irony can serve as a corrective to fallacies, hypocrisy, prejudice, ignorance or simple inno-cence in a world viewed as fundamentally logical. Muecke called irony in that context *Specific Irony*. In contrast, the world itself, or aspects of it, can be seen as fundamentally and inescapably ironic. Muecke called irony in that world view *General Irony*. The General Ironist has a distinctive point of view but still shares the predicament of the *alazons* who are unaware of the irony.

The ironist/audience and *alazon* roles can also be described in relation to event scripts. The observers (ironist/audience) see the ironic anomaly the script, whether or not they themselves are implicated. The *alazon* does not. The *alazon* is key because script anomalies may be simply surprising or incomprehensible—not ironic—without the concept that someone would not "get" the irony (Muecke, 1969). The existence of the *alazon* dis-tinguishes the structure of irony, provides its judgmental edge and gives ironic thought its particular creative significance. The ironic insight is not simply idiosyncratic. It is significant specifically because it undermines existing and plausible assumptions about the situation. The originality is inherently juxtaposed to at least someone's beliefs in the domain.

The roles inherent to ironic situations were also important to Shaw's thinking about WWI. In the first two pages of *Common Sense* (1914/1931) Shaw, ever the director, laid out the key roles for the stream of ironic predicaments and solutions that he would be describing. In the opening lines he defined the audience by directly addressing the "more thoughtful of us" (p. 19) with the imperative that it was time to think sanely about the war. This audience was then distinguished from "the thoughtless" (*alazons*) with a generous dose of verbal irony:

> As to the thoughtless, well, not for a moment dare I suggest that for the first few weeks they were all scared out of their wits; for I know too well that the British civilian does not allow his perfect courage to be questioned: only experienced soldiers and foreigners are allowed the infirmity of fear. But they were—shall I say a little upset? They felt in that solemn hour that England was lost if only one single traitor in their midst let slip the truth about anything in the universe (1914/1931, p. 19).

With both the audience and *alazon* specified, the only role left was that of the ironist. As author, pointing out the ironies, Shaw was already cast, but he made his role explicit. Shaw specifically described himself as an Irishman who had the detached perspective of a foreigner and "perhaps a slightly malicious taste" (1914/1931, p. 19) for taking the conceit out of England. Because he was Irish, his own prejudices about the war would be different than "those which blind the British patriot" (p. 20).

In spite of Shaw's attention to these roles, the reactions to *Common Sense* indicated that his readers did not take their assigned positions on cue. One reason was, no doubt, that many readers were indeed "scared out of their wits." Among the roles offered, they felt more like the scared *alazons* than the "thoughtful" audience. In case readers did not identify with the *alazons* on the first page, they soon would. As the ironies played out in the text of *Common Sense*, Shaw described a broad range of *alazons*, ultimately indicting most readers. Of course, such confrontation was typically Shavian.

Shaw's introduction of his Irish identity was less characteristic, and that move further undermined the initial delineation of roles. The thoughtful audience he needed to reach was not Irish, but English. In one stroke of the pen he had separated the English into the thoughtful audience and the thoughtless *alazons*; in the next stroke he lumped them together as simply English.

Principle 3: Irony is a Conceptual Structure

We can now define the basic structure of irony more precisely as a script anomaly juxtaposed with an *alazon's* expectations. The Junker passage of *Common Sense* (1914/1931)again provides an example for analysis. As Shaw listed specific British government leaders who were Junkers, he highlighted Winston Churchill for his "frank anti-German pugnacity" (p. 22). Then Shaw contrasted Churchill's pugnacious stance to the peace rhetoric that the government had actually used before the war. Shaw speculated that if Churchill had conducted pre-war diplomacy, "he might quite possibly have averted the war (and thereby greatly disappointed himself and the British public)" (p. 32). Table 1 shows a structural analysis of this situation, relating behaviors to goals as in event scripts, with designated *alazons*.

The structure of ironic thought is not the entire picture, however.

Principle 4: Irony is a Perceptual Dynamic

The world is rife with *alazony* as indicated or implied by contradictions, confusion, fallacies, hypocrisy and absurdity. And every situation can be described from multiple perspectives—one man's prophecy is another's

TABLE 1.　Structure of overt irony in Shaw's description of Churchill's prewar rhetoric

Alazons: Churchill and British Public		
Expected Event Script:		
Intention	*Means or Behavior*	*Outcome*
To fight	Pugnacious rhetoric	War
Situation Described:		
Intention	*Means or Behavior*	*Outcome*
To fight	Pugnacious rhetoric	War is averted

lunacy. As a result, an observer can perceive "latent irony" (Muecke, 1969, p. 82) in almost any situation. The observer just has to have some sophistication, particular motivation and ironic sensibility.

These three elements—sophistication, motivation and sensibility—are standard fare among current theories of irony, but I am placing particular emphasis on their roles in ironic perception. Linda Hutcheon (1994) has theorized that irony "happens" (p. 58) for a person when an experience "rubs together" (p. 19) different perspectives with which the person is familiar. Shaw (1949) seemed to agree. He described his own unique perceptions as cognitive thunderbolts: "Every subject struck my mind at an angle that produced reflections new to my audience" (p. 57). I am proposing a way of thinking about the point of view that facilitates such thunderbolts.

First, perception of irony requires some sophistication about the situation (Frye, 1957/1990; Muecke, 1969; Rorty, 1989; Hutcheon, 1994). The ironist cannot perceive twists to event scripts if she does not know the situation. The more she knows, the subtler her irony can be. *Common Sense* is an outstanding example of sophistication as a foundation for irony. One of the most striking elements of Shaw's essay is the level of detail about European history and international diplomacy which he provided as context for his ironic insights.

Second, the ironist is motivated. She wants to juxtapose different perspectives. Irony can serve many diverse functions from including particular people to excluding them; from exploring new perspectives to obscuring one's own position; from ingratiating oneself to attacking others; from adding humor to deepening seriousness; from diffusing conflict to intensifying it (Hutcheon, 1994[2]). But even the most benign use of ironic humor to defuse conflict involves a differentiation between "us," who can step back and see the humor, from at least a hypothetical "them," who cannot.

---

[2] For a particularly interesting discussion of the range of ironic functions, as well as a useful schematic of selected functions, see pp. 44–56.

I propose this motivation in lieu of the often cited ironic "detachment." Shaw's case demonstrates the insufficiency of detachment as a description of an ironic point of view. Yes, Shaw himself emphasized that, as an Irishman, he had a detached perspective on the conflict. But, in reality, his attitude toward the war was anything but detached. His attempts to influence British war policy were one of the most passionate, challenging and frustrating undertakings of Shaw's life. Passionate irony might be particular to Shaw or Swift or Voltaire or Shakespeare or Baudelaire, but the demands of ironic perception imply otherwise. The rubbing together of perspectives that occurs in irony—as well as the knowledge about the situation that is required—indicate a form of complex engagement, not detachment. In its more defensive functions, irony may make the speaker appear aloof, but a truly detached stance should lead to withdrawal from the situation (literally "detaching"), not ironic engagement.

Shaw might have better described his Irish perspective as *distinctive*. His point of view was distinct enough to juxtapose with prevailing opinion. He was also motivated to make that juxtaposition. He *wanted* to redefine social and conceptual boundaries—the lines between us and them and the lines between is and is not.

Finally, the ironist has to have an ironic sensibility—an awareness that there might be an ironic way to see the situation. Such an awareness probably develops along multiple dimensions. Certain individuals, like Shaw, are known for their sense or irony. Shaw's case tends to support the view that childhood experiences contribute to ironic sensibility. He remembered learning his particular humor when he was very young, from his father (Shaw, 1949). Shaw was also influenced as a child by his "Rabelaisian" uncle Walter and his mother's strongly non-conformist attitudes (Shaw, 1949; Holroyd, 1988). Overlapping the story of the individual's development are cultural dimensions. Remember that Lucariello (1994) concluded from her research that various forms of irony are culturally recognized. Therefore, most people within a given culture should have some ability to recognize irony. In addition, certain cultures seem to emphasize irony more than others. For example, the Irish are known for their extensive use of irony. This cultural influence probably helped make Shaw's ironic sensibility particularly keen, as it probably did that of his fellow countrymen, such as Swift and Wilde.

With sophistication, motivation and sensibility, irony can "happen" for the individual. The perceptual dynamic can then continue as the observer re-presents the situation with an ironic "wink." The ironist may thereby stimulate the ironic perception of others. Aha! They see the irony as well. Or ... they do not "get it," or they see irony, but not the irony that the initial observer intended (Hutcheon, 1994). In other words, the audience's knowledge, motivation and sensibility have to align to some degree with those of the ironist to facilitate further irony.

Such alignments, or misalignments, can vary widely. As a result, ironic perceptions from a given situation can take on multiple lives—in different variations with different audiences. Furthermore, as we will see in Shaw's thinking, one ironic perception can lead to others within a single observer's thought. Thus, the ironic dynamic occurs both within thought and within groups, cognitively and socially.

If we could take a minds-eye snap-shot of irony when it "happens," we would see the ironic structure of meaning described earlier. Beyond that basic structure, the particularities of any given irony would correspond to an entry on one of the many typologies that the long tradition of structural analysis has produced (e.g., Muecke, 1969; Booth, 1974; Wilde, 1981; Lucariello, 1994). The ironies in our minds-eye photos might include Socratic Irony, ingénue irony (emperor's new clothes), ironic dilemmas, sharp aesthetic juxtapositions, role-reversals, Catch-22s, stable or unstable irony, premodern, modern or postmodern irony...

All irony involves both structure and dynamic. Which aspect is most apparent depends in part on whether we are looking at overt or covert irony. As I will describe, the dynamic aspects of ironic perception become particularly illuminating at the covert end of the irony spectrum. The identification of ironic structures is easiest at the overt end, where the "wink" is hard to miss. The conventional markers of overt verbal irony and the structures of explicit descriptions of ironic situations allow strong arguments for both ironic intention and interpretation. We can follow the clues in the text, verify the structures and, thereby, identify the irony. Our examination of Shaw's thinking about the war begins with his extensive overt irony. But even that task is not easy.

THE COMPLEXITY AND "LOGIC" OF SHAW'S IRONY

One challenge to identifying Shaw's use of overt irony is its very pervasiveness. In a quantitative study of Shaw's ironic thinking about WWI, I found that Shaw's thinking as expressed in *Common Sense* involved descriptions of hundreds of situational ironies (Hanchett Hanson, 1999[3]).

---

[3] Using a methodology in keeping with the principles that have been outlined here, this study identified 306 distinct situation ironies, .88 per 100 words, in the entire text of *Common Sense* (interrater reliability, 80%). *Distinct situational ironies* were based on the count of all situational ironies identified, less those coded as *examples only* of ironic principles already stated and counted within the discussion of a particular topic.

In the first few pages of *Common Sense* (1914/1931), Shaw described the war as an ironic twist on the standard war script. In attacking what was believed to be the foreign characteristics of the enemy, each side was actually attacking an aspect of itself. The English, who were supposed to be fighting Junkers and militarists, were also being led by Junkers and militarists. This led to a further, more cutting or tragic irony. In fighting this war, the people on each side were actually strengthening what they detested—the Junkers and militarists—in their own societies. Thus, one ironic insight was the basis of the next. After describing those two ironies, Shaw moved to the "remedy":

> No doubt the heroic remedy for this tragic misunderstanding is that both armies should shoot their officers and go home to gather in their harvests in the villages and make a revolution in the towns...But there is no chance—or, as our Junkers would put it, no danger—of our soldiers yielding to such an ecstasy of common sense (p. 20).

Here is another example of verbal irony as condensed reference to situation scripts. Linking the term "heroic" to shooting superior officers and to the daily work of the harvest (overstatement); using the term "misunderstanding" for the war itself (understatement); linking revolution to common sense and then the very concept of an "ecstasy of common sense" (stylistic placing) are all techniques of verbal irony (Muecke, 1969). Note that none of this irony was necessary to make the logical argument for a solution. That argument: the people of Germany and England should insist that their governments withdraw from the war and focus on domestic reforms. The verbal irony added edge. It also evoked an array of event scripts and, thereby, contributed to the flow of the argument.

The "heroic" reference re-evoked the standard war script in which heroism plays a key role. The "misunderstanding" reference then implied a more intimate communication script, or a more local political script, where misunderstandings would be standard fare. Then dropping in the reference to revolution, took the situation to another extreme of political conflict.

Here, Shaw did not just add a single ironic twist to a standard event script. He evoked and juxtaposed multiple scripts. That juxtaposition set up a spectrum of perspectives for considering the implications of the proposed remedy. At one end, the remedy amounted to revolution for the existing powers; at the other, it dramatized the possibility of neighborly recognition of mutual interests between England and Germany. In between was the actual fighting force, the soldiers who could conceivably redirect their energy to a different concept of heroism and, thereby, bring about the remedy. Here we see a type of ironic "logic," in which irony went beyond questioning assumptions and provided frameworks for exploring a concept.

THE EVOLUTION OF SHAW'S IRONIC PERSPECTIVE

In 1919 Shaw wrote "Heartbreak House and Horseback Hall" the preface to *Heartbreak House*. As he had in *Common Sense*, Shaw analyzed the causes and impacts of the war, using irony as extensively as he had in 1914 (Hanchett Hanson, 1999[4]). But the preface to *Heartbreak House* reflected a different ironic point of view. The first clue to this shift was that roles were not assigned so clearly up front in the *Heartbreak House* preface as they had been in *Common Sense*. In particular, Shaw's role as ironist was not as stable. At several points in the initial pages of "Heartbreak House and Horseback Hall," he used "we" in describing the *alazons'* perspective. At one point later in the essay ("The Sufferings of the Sane"), he described himself explicitly as a victim of the situation. Everyone seemed to be victims of the irony—Shaw was, after all, looking back on a world war.

In other words, there was a shift in the specific motivation that contributed to Shaw's perceptual dynamic, a shift in the problem he was trying to solve. Making sense of the horror that Europe had been through and contemplating a future after that experience was very different from trying to influence international policies in 1914. Ironic thinking still applied. Just as he had in the early months of the war, in 1919 Shaw juxtaposed what he saw as blind, foolish and self-centered perspectives with the possibility of political wisdom. But looking back, after the war, everyone shared the *alazon's* predicament. Given human nature, it had all been inevitable. After the conflict, no one was in the now hypothetical seat of political wisdom.

We commonly call such perspectives cosmic irony, irony of fate or self-irony—world views in which at least certain ironies are inescapable. As previously mentioned, Muecke (1969) called these world views General Irony. Like Western culture as a whole, at the end of the war Shaw was

---

[4] Only the first 23 topics of "Heartbreak House and Horseback Hall" (1919c) were analyzed because the remaining topics focused on the roles of theater in politics, which had not been addressed in *Common Sense*. Compared to the .88 distinct situational ironies per 100 words in *Common Sense*, .89 per 100 words were found in the first 23 topics of the *Heartbreak House* preface (interrater reliability, 81%).

confronting the failure of his 19th-century faith in progress. In Shaw's case this ironic thinking was a shift in perspective, but still creative. As Holroyd (1988) has observed, "Shaw's prejudice was optimism" (p. 41). That observation would hold true even as Shaw confronted new depths of despair over the human condition. The Shavian life force would ultimately use this challenge as a springboard to new terrain.

A series of ironies, described at the beginning of the *Heartbreak House* preface, illustrate Shaw's perspective in 1919. As Table 2 shows, Shaw began by describing an ironic relationship between politicians and the cultured upper class (the inhabitants of "Heartbreak House"). Hannibal's army had been innervated by the luxuries of Capua and, in like manner, Shaw saw the country house culture of prewar leisured Europe as a Capua for politicians. This reference was particularly pointed for Fabians. No longer were the heirs of Quintus Fabius Maximus fighting Hannibal. Instead, they contributed to the destruction of their own polity by following in Hannibal's footsteps. From there, Shaw's scope widened. In the next topic the irony included all of the upper classes. Then Shaw described ironies resulting from English democracy, culminating in a view of that system as self-defeating. In the next topic, "Nature's Long Credits," he described the ironies leading to the war as humanity's relationship to Nature as a whole.

Here, the ironists of the initial, narrower contexts became the *alazons* of the later, broader ones. The critique of *Heartbreak House* became itself naïve in a system that would not let the *Heartbreak House* inhabitants participate, if they had wanted. Then laying blame on the country's political system became naïve if Nature itself laid a trap that humanity was unable to avoid.

In this progression, the last topic—"Nature's Long Credits"—was both culminating and provisional. The metaphor of Nature setting a trap for humanity tends to indicate inevitable irony. Nature's role of creditor to humanity's reckless spending, however, implied that the situation was correctable. Shaw was explicit on that point: "[The plagues of war] were all as preventable as the great Plague of London, and came solely because they had not been prevented" (1919c, p. xv). More caution would prevent the tragic irony, but humanity gave no evidence of being capable of that degree of caution.

In effect, Shaw had been reluctantly dragged into General (inevitable) Irony territory, but he still clutched the Specific (correctable) Irony flag. If human nature led to inevitably tragic ironies, then the solution was to change human nature. Shaw would present proposals to just that end in his next major work, *Back to Methuselah: A Metabiological Pentateuch* (1921/1977).

TABLE 2. "Heartbreak House and Horseback Hall" (1919c): Progression of expanding ironic contexts

1 Ironic outcome for politicians	2 Ironic dilemma	3 Ironic means of English politics	4 Ironic outcomes of democracy	5 Ironic means of nature
"For prime ministers and their like, it [Heartbreak House] was a veritable Capua" (p. xi).	"so the prime minister folk had to choose between barbarism [aristocrats of Horseback Hall] and Capua. And of the two atmospheres it is hard to say which was the more fatal to statesmanship" (pp. xi–xii).	"The barbarians were not only literally in the saddle, but on the front bench in the House of Commons, with nobody to correct their incredible ignorance of modern thought and political science but upstarts from the counting-house, who had spent their lives furnishing their pockets instead of their minds" (pp. xi–xii).	"Not that they [the inhabitants of Heartbreak House] would have been allowed to meddle anyhow, as only through accident of being a hereditary peer can anyone in these days of Votes for Everybody get into parliament if handicapped by serious modern cultural equipment" (p. xiii).	"Nature's way of dealing with unhealthy conditions is unfortunately not one that compels us to conduct a solvent hygiene on a cash basis. She demoralizes us with long credits and reckless overdrafts, and then pulls us up cruelly with catastrophic bankruptcies (p. xiv).

IMPACT OF SHAW'S NETWORK OF ENTERPRISE

In studying cases of exceptional creativity, Gruber (1974/1981, 1989) has found that the creative person's network of enterprise is a useful construct, representing the creative person's purpose and distinctive point of view over time. The network of enterprise consists of ongoing, long-term activities that develop as interlocking systems so that changes in one part of the system ultimately affect the rest of the system.

Shaw's intellectual and creative development after the war is a particularly good example of Gruber's concept of the interdependence of a creative person's enterprises. The frustration that Shaw encountered in advancing the ideas he had developed in his war enterprise led to two plays, *Heartbreak House* (1919d) and *Back to Methuselah* (1921/1977). In *Heartbreak House* he looked back, saw his own contributions to the problems he had defined and reframed those problems as broadly human, rather than simply political. Those changes in his political perspective reinvigorated another important

Shavian concept, creative evolution. Shaw contended that Nature, as life force, was driven to improve itself through humanity. This philosophy was a remix of the 19th-century scripts for religion, progress and evolution. Like a Hegelian God, Nature realized itself through its creation. Furthermore, the 19th-century faith in progress was preserved. By choosing Lamark's theory of evolution, instead of Darwin's, however, Shaw replaced the blind struggle for survival with a drive to perfection. He replaced Darwinian war with Nietzschean will.

Before WWI, Shaw's most extensive treatment of his idea of the life force was in the play *Man and Superman* (1903/1942) and its preface. Shaw expanded on this philosophy with *Back to Methuselah* (1921/1977) a play in five parts, plus a preface. The second part of the play portrayed an informal, drawing-room meeting among politicians and scientists after WWI. There, Shaw laid out the need for humanity to evolve to a state where it does not act so childishly to such tragic ends. The solution: the human life span needed to be prolonged to at least 300 years so that people could, in effect, grow up within their lifetimes. The next three parts of the play portrayed that evolution occurring. Shaw, thereby, continued his consideration of the irony of "Nature's Long Credits" (see Table 2) and how it could be avoided. In the highest ironic tradition, *Methuselah* was at once fanciful and deadly serious.

IRONY'S MANY LIVES

So far, I have focused on the structure of Shaw's ironic thinking and the internal dynamic of that thought. The external dynamic is, of course, also critical to the story. Shaw's overt description of ironic situations may be relatively clear evidence of his perceptions. *He* perceived irony in the situations he described, but, despite his efforts, most of his readers did not.

Wells' (1914) description of *Common Sense* as "distorting, discrediting, confusing" (p. 6) was a clear indication that the irony Shaw perceived was not evident to Wells. Fellow author Henry Arthur Jones published an open letter to Shaw in response to *Common Sense* that included the tirade: "Mischief was your midwife and Misrule your nurse, and Unreason brought you up at her feet—no other ancestry and rearing had you" (Weintraub, 1971, p. 60). This circumstance went beyond the cases that Hutcheon (1994) has analyzed and to which cognitive psychologists have given much attention—cases where an audience does not *get* the irony. By 1914 Shaw was famous throughout the world. H. G. Wells was particularly familiar with the Shavian style. Wells first heard Shaw speak on a street corner in the 1880s, and had been a member of the Fabian Society from 1903–1908 (Ervine, 1956). Furthermore, Shaw's intentions were well marked in his texts. Still, many in Shaw's audience saw his descriptions as distortion, confusion and unreason—not ironic insight.

Today's appreciation (with hindsight) of Shaw's ironic perceptions is also evidence of irony's external dynamic—the role that the audience plays in determining whether or not irony "happens." The difference between 1914 and the beginning of the 21st century is not just that we have greater ironic sensibility, although we may. We no doubt miss much of Shaw's covert irony because we lack the sophistication of readers who were following the news and hearing everyday rumors as the war unfolded. We miss much of the sharpness of Shaw's ironic edge as well. For example, the portrayal of Sir Edward Grey as *alazon*, bungling English diplomacy leading to the war, was explicit in *Common Sense*. Today, we get Shaw's point, but for us Grey is abstract, rather than a specific person. He is not *our* leader. We do not feel the edge of the irony as we might if we were English in 1914. The 1914 audience felt the force of the ironic reframing much more acutely as an attack on their leadership when they *were* "scared out of their wits," going into the war. Without our historical distance, Shaw's original audience was extremely sensitive to irony's edge, and—ironically—that made it difficult to contemplate.

LESSONS

The external dynamic of irony means that this research is itself an artifact of the 20th-century legacy of irony. As Fussell (1975/2000) has contended, the Great War may have contributed significantly to current ironic points of view, but there have also been other contributions. Americans have had Vietnam to undercut our *alazony*. Our sense of irony has been influenced by other factors as well, ranging from 19th-century Romanticism (Muecke, 1969) to 20th-century post-modernism (Hutcheon, 1988) and current media culture (Baudrillard, 1983/1993; de Zengotita, 2002). Still, we are faced with the fact that, in studying Shaw's irony, we are in reality studying a relationship between his intent and the points of view of our own culture and time. Within that reality, what do we learn?

After the terrorist attacks on the United States on September 11, 2001, journalist Roger Rosenblatt (2001) declared "the death" of the irony of American intellectuals for whom, he contended, "nothing was to be believed in or taken seriously. Nothing was real. With a giggle and a smirk, our chattering classes—our columnists and pop culture makers—declared that detachment and personal whimsy were the necessary tools for an oh-so-cool life. Who but a slobbering bumpkin would think, 'I feel your pain'?" (p. 79). Thus, we hear 21st-century echoes of H. G. Wells' (1914) condemnation of "those perpetual children who live in a dream world of make-believe ... It is almost as if there was no pain in all the world" (p. 6).

In spite of the similarities in these critiques, our world differs significantly from Wells' world. At the beginning of the 21st century, global economics, communication and culture are vastly more integrated than they were in 1914. Indeed, constant and unavoidable encounters with different perspectives may contribute to our emphasis on irony. Still, like Shaw's readers in 1914, when we feel threatened, we are understandably tempted to demonize the enemy, divide the world into "good" and "evil" and throw out the complexity of ironic thought.

As previously discussed, another difference between 1914 and today is our concept of irony. Wells attacked a single man for his views and did not mention the word "irony"; whereas, Rosenblatt attacked a whole class of people, specifically for their emphasis on irony. Earlier, I explained that we could look at much of Shaw's ironic thinking as a combination of certain definitions of paradox and wit. I now qualify that statement, for I also believe that our current concept of irony has distinct advantages. Today's irony goes beyond the endless loop associated with paradox, and, therefore, accommodates solutions more readily. And, although irony may juxtapose frivolous with serious perspectives, it does not lean so strongly toward the frivolous as does wit. Rosenblatt's critique shows that, today, even the critics of irony take it seriously.

In this context, I believe that Shaw's insights concerning WWI are instructive for us. Whatever the uncertainties facing our culture now or in the future, we should appreciate our hard-won and broad concept of irony. That concept provides a lens on a particular way of thinking creatively, one way of questioning assumptions and searching for new solutions. Furthermore, as Shaw's case demonstrates, irony is not necessarily just a detour, however fruitful, from nonironic thinking. It can also be a driving force in thought with its own "logic," providing frameworks for exploring ideas.

I am not contending that irony is infallible. The ironic point of view is not necessarily right, and, by definition, cannot be the rule. Nor can we simply go back to Shaw's solutions as we face our own conflicts. Irony by today's standards is always specific to context (the element of sophistication) and unexpected (a twist on current event scripts).

For those very reasons, it is important to include ironic points of view in our deliberations, especially when the need for creative solutions is urgent. Twenty-first-century situations like the U.S. led "war" on terrorism, the vicissitudes of a global economy and the rapid growth of worldwide communication—not to mention the explosion of human population accompanied by dramatic demographic shifts—all include unexpected

challenges that can be perceived as ironic. Much of the creative thinking
that will go into meeting such challenges may also be ironic.

REFERENCES

Ankersmit, F. R. (1996). *Aesthetic politics: Political philosophy beyond fact and value*. Stanford CA:
    Sanford University Press.
Aristotle (1990). *Nichomachean ethics*. Cambridge MA: Harvard University Press.
Ashcraft, M. H. (1989). *Human memory and cognition*. Glenview, IL: Scott, Foresman.
Auden, W. H. (1942/1953). The Fabian Figaro. In L. Kronenberger (Ed.), *George Bernard Shaw:
    A critical survey* (pp. 153–157). New York: The World Publishing Company.
Baudrillard, J. (1983/1993). The procession of simulacra. In J. Natoli & L. Hutcheon (Eds.),
    A postmodern reader (pp. 342–375). Albany: State University of New York.
Bloom, H. (1987). Introduction. In H. Bloom (Ed.), *George Bernard Shaw* (pp. 2–25). New York:
    Chelsea House.
Booth, W. C. (1974). *A rhetoric of irony*. Chicago: University of Chicago Press.
Bransford, J. D. (1979). *Human cognition: Learning remembering and understanding*. Belmont CA:
    Wadsworth.
Brooks, C. (1947). *The well wrought urn*. New York: Harcourt.
Chesterton, G. K. (1909/1953). The critic. In L. Kronenberger (Ed.), *George Bernard Shaw: A
    critical survey* (pp. 26–37). New York: The World Publishing Company.
Corrigan, R. W. (1959). Heartbreak House: Shaw's elegy for Europe. *The Shaw Review*, II, ix,
    2–6.
De Man, P. (1979). *Allegories of reading: Figural language in Rousseau, Nietzsche, Rilke, and Proust*.
    New Haven: Yale Univeristy Press.
De Zengotita , T. (2002, April). The Numbing of the American Mind. *Harper's*, 304, 33–40.
Dent, A. (Ed.). (1952). *Bernard Shaw and Mrs. Patrick Campbell: Their correspondence* (p. 209).
    New York: Alfred A. Knopf.
Ervine, S. (1956). *Bernard Shaw: His life, work and friends*. New York: William Marrow.
Freud, S. (1905/1960). *Jokes and their relation to the unconscious*. New York: W. W. Norton & Co.
Frye, N. (1957/1990). *Anatomy of criticism: Four essays*. Princeton & Oxford: Princeton Univer-
    sity Press.
Fussell, P. (1975/2000). *The Great War and modern memory*. Oxford: Oxford Univeristy Press.
Gibbs, R. W. Jr. (1994). *The poetics of mind*. Cambridge, England: Cambridge University
    Press.
Gruber, H. E. (1989). The evolving systems approach to creative work. In D. B. Wallace &
    H. E. Gruber (Eds.), *Creative people at work: Twelve cognitive case studies*. (pp. 3–24). New
    York: Oxford University Press.
Gruber, H. E. (1974/1981). *Darwin on man: A psychological study of scientific creativity*. Chicago:
    University of Chicago Press.
Gruber, H. E. (1978). Darwin's "Tree of Nature" and other images of wide scope. In J. Wechsler
    (Ed.), *On aesthetics in science* (pp. 121–140). Cambridge, MA: MIT Press.
Hanchett Hanson, M. (1999). *Irony, conflict and creativity: A case study of the creative development
    of George Bernard Shaw as an ironist during WWI*. Ph.D. dissertation, Columbia University.
Holroyd, M. (1991). *Bernard Shaw: The pursuit of power*. New York: Random House.
Holroyd, M. (1988). *Bernard Shaw: The search for love*. New York: Random House.
Hutcheon, L. (1994). *Irony's edge*. New York: Routledge.
Hutcheon, L. (1988). *A poetics of postmodernism: History, theory, fiction*. New York: Routledge.

Kreuz, R. J. (2000). The production and processing of verbal irony. *Metaphor and Symbol, 15,* 99–107.

Kumon-Nakamura, S., Glucksberg, S., & Brown, M. (1995). How about another piece of pie: The allusional pretense theory of discourse irony. *Journal of Experimental Psychology: General, 124,* 3–21.

Laurence, D. H. (Ed.). (1988). *Bernard Shaw: Collected letters 1926–1950.* London: Max Reinhardt, Ltd.

Laurence, D. H. (Ed.). (1985). *Bernard Shaw: Collected letters 1911–1925* (pp. 536–537; 546). London: Max Reinhardt, Ltd.

Lemert, C. (1992). General social theory, irony, postmodernism. In S. Seidman and D. G. Wagner (Eds.), *Postmodernism and social theory.* Cambridge MA and Oxford: Blackwell.

Lucariello, J. (1994). Situational irony: a concept of events gone awry. *Journal of Experimental Psychology: General, 123,* 129–145.

Lurariello, J. & Mindolvich, C. (1995). The devlopment of complex metarepresentational reasoning. The case of situational irony. *Cognitive Development, 10,* 551–576.

Mayne, E. (1967). *The wit and satire of Bernard Shaw.* Guildford, UK and London: Billing & Sons Limited.

Meisel, M. (1971/1987). Shaw and revolution: The politics of the plays. In Harold Bloom (Ed.), *Modern critical views: George Bernard Shaw* (pp. 99–119). Chelsea House Publishers: New York.

Muecke, D. C. (1969). *The Compass of Irony.* London: Metheun.

Osowski, J. G. (1989). Ensembles of metaphor in the psychology of William James. In D. B. Wallace & H. E. Gruber (Eds.), *Creative people at work: Twelve cognitive case studies,* (pp. 127–145). New York: Oxford University Press.

Rorty, R. (1989). *Contingency, irony and solidarity.* Cambridge, UK: Cambridge University Press.

Rosenblatt, R. (2001). The age of irony comes to an end. *Time Magazine, 158,* 79, September 24.

Royal.gov.uk (2002). History of the monarchy: Saxe-Coburg-Gotha. [Online.] Available at: www.royal.gov.uk/output/Page128.asp

Schank, R. C. & Abelson, R. (1977). *Scripts, plans, goals and understanding.* Hillsdale, NJ: Erlbaum.

Shaw, G. B. (1898/1980a). *Mrs. Warren's profession. Plays unpleasant.* Middlesex, England: Penguin Books, Ltd.

Shaw, G. B. (1898/1980b). Preface: Mainly about myself. *Plays unpleasant.* Middlesex, England: Penguin Books, Ltd.

Shaw, G. B. (1898/1980c). *The philanderer. Plays unpleasant.* Middlesex, England: Penguin Books, Ltd.

Shaw, G. B. (1921/1977). *Back to Methuselah: A metabiological pentateuch.* New York: Penguin.

Shaw, G. B. (1916/1973). *Pygmalion.* New York: Washington Square Press.

Shaw, G. B. (1894/1960). *Arms and the man.* New York: The New American Library.

Shaw, G. B. (1891/1955). The Messiah again. In Eric Bentley (Ed.), *Shaw on music: A selection of music criticism of Bernard Shaw made by Eric Bentley.* Garden City, NY: Doubleday & Company, Inc.

Shaw, G. B. (1949). *Sixteen self sketches.* London: Constable and Company Limited.

Shaw, G. B. (1903/1942). *Man and superman.* New York: Dodd, Mead & Co.

Shaw, G. B. (1898/1942). *Caesar and Cleopatra: A history.* New York: Dodd, Mead & Company.

Shaw, G. B. (1899/1941). *Captain Brassbound's conversion: An adventure.* New York: Dodd, Mead & Company.

Shaw, G. B. (1898/1941). *The Man of destiny.* New York: Dodd, Mead & Company.

Shaw, G. B. (1914/1931). Common sense about the war. In *What I really wrote about the war.* New York: Brentano.

Shaw, G. B. (1913/1931). Armaments and conscription: A triple alliance against war. In *What I really wrote about the war*. New York: Brentano.

Shaw, G. B. (1919a). *Annajanska, the Bolshevik empress*. In *Heartbreak House, Great Catherine, and playlets of the war*, pp. 275–295. New York: Brentano.

Shaw, G. B. (1919b). *Augustus does his bit*. In *Heartbreak House, Great Catherine, and playlets of the war*, pp. 247–272. New York: Brentano.

Shaw, G. B. (1919c). Heartbreak house and horseback hall. In *Heartbreak House, Great Catherine, and playlets of the war*, pp. ix–lv. New York: Brentano.

Shaw, G. B. (1919d). *Heartbreak house*. In *Heartbreak House, Great Catherine, and playlets of the war*, pp. 1–122. New York: Brentano.

Shaw, G. B. (1919e). *The Inca of Perusalem*. In *Heartbreak House, Great Catherine, and playlets of the war*, pp. 213–243. New York: Brentano.

Shaw, G. B. (1919f). *O'Flaherty, V.C.* In *Heartbreak House, Great Catherine, and playlets of the war*, pp. 179–209. New York: Brentano.

Shaw, G. B. (1900). *Fabianism and empire: A manifesto by the Fabian Society*. London: G. Richards.

Sperber D., & Wilson, D. (1995). *Relevance: Communication and cognition* (2nd ed.). Cambridge, MA: Blackwell.

Stringfellow, F., Jr. (1994). *The meaning of irony: A psychoanalytic investigation*. Albany: State University of New York Press.

Venturi, R. (1977). *Complexity and contradiction in architecture* (2nd edition). New York: The Museum of Modern Art.

Weintraub (1966/1970). The avant-garde Shaw. In W. D. Smith (Ed.), *Bernard Shaw's Plays* (pp. 341–355). New York: W. W. Norton & Co.

Weintraub (1971). *Journey to heartbreak: The crucible years of Bernard Shaw 1914–1918*. New York: Weybright and Talley.

Wegner, D. M. (1994). Ironic processes of mental control. *Psychological Review*, 101, 34–52.

Wells, H. G. (1914). Muddle-headedness and Russia. *The Daily Chronicle*, December 31, p. 6.

White, H. (1973). *Metahistory: The historical imagination in nineteenth-century Europe*. Baltimore, MD: Johns Hopkins University Press.

Wilde, A. (1981). *Horizons of ascent: Modernism, postmodernism and the ironic imagination*. Baltimore: Johns Hopkins University Press.

Wingfield-Stratford, E. (1968). What really happened. In George A. Panichas (Ed.), *Promise of Greatness: The war of 1914–1918* (pp. 380–398). New York: John Day Company.

Winner, E. (1988). *The point of words: Children's understanding of metaphor and irony*. Cambridge, MA: Harvard University Press.

3

VALUES AND THE ROMANCE NOVEL
JOURNEYS OF THE READER

Sara N. Davis

> Inevitably we are drawn to thinking in terms of a social process, dia-
> logue, as the meeting ground on which new questions are raised, the
> mating ground on which new combinations are found, and the testing
> ground in which novelties are critically evaluated and assimilated into
> the body of shared knowledge and thought. (Gruber, 1994, p. 14).[1]

The research presented in this chapter examines the ways in which reader
responses are constructed in dialogue with cultural discourses. These provide the context when students read romance novels. Readers enter the
process with many negative evaluations of romance novels which conflict
with other prevalent discourses valuing romance for women. While much
previous research emphasized the impact of textual structures and content
in the reader/text interaction, the study presented here shows how the
knowledge of the reader plays a crucial role in constructing meaning.

My initial work examined the evolution of responses of a reader over
the course of several readings of a single text. My research goal was to chart
the interaction between reader and text in the developing response to a
literary text. I was interested in the ways in which the reader's own intellectual and personal history served as a lens through which she organized

[1] I would like to thank Howard Gruber who provided the inspiration for this research.

textual elements. How did she both interpret the text in the manner of her intellectual community and respond out of the wellspring of her own accumulated life history? The theoretical underpinning of this work is derived from the evolving systems approach developed by Gruber (1989) and especially from three of his ideas. These are: the importance of viewing ideas in context; understanding the evolution of ideas and perspectives; and looking at how elements in any situation interact. My concern in the work presented here is with the ways context affects understanding.

THE STUDY

In this study, I develop ideas regarding context, focusing on the influence of general cultural imperatives on the reader/text interaction. I am concerned with the ways in which cultural constraints condition a reader's experience. This has necessitated a shift from a focus on the responses of individual readers to examination of larger numbers of readers. For several years, I have been interested in the cultural constraints surrounding the reception of romance novels. In order to understand the ways in which the reader and text interact, one also has to develop an understanding of who that reader is as a result of the cultural and intellectual communities with which she has participated. In this research my goal is to define some of the contextual constraints that govern the interaction with the text. Romance novels are ideal material for this endeavor because they present an intersection of several conflicting cultural discourses. They are highly popular and widely read at the same time that they are disparaged and shunned.

I will describe the ways in which romance novels are embedded in a variety of prevalent social discourses and how these affect the reception processes of readers. Because ideas regarding the status and merit of romance novels are so widespread, they enter the consciousness even of non-readers. An analysis of these cultural discourses permits an investigation into the ways readers construct meaning in accord with these existing ideas. The cultural discourse provides perspectives on the novels themselves, implications about the types of people who read them, ideas about the status of romance in the lives of women.

I use the term discourse here to represent a set of widely-held ideas that have arisen through social constructions that function in the public realm. These ideas are sufficiently powerful to shape thought processes. The discourses situate the reader in relation to a text. They frame how readers view romance novels, how they view the readers of these books, and how they believe they will be defined by others who know they are readers. As readers proceed through the process, from anticipating and purchasing, reading and responding, and reflecting and evaluating upon both their experience and what these books mean in their culture, they are measuring their ideas and reactions against the major discourses that frame the experience. It is clear that readers are also weighing their individual impressions against these broad-based cultural assumptions. Thus, readers' experiences are shaped by the cultural discourse as well as by idiosyncratic experiences.

INTRODUCTION

Historically, scholars were interested in how texts influence readers. The meaning was seen as residing in the text and it was the task of the reader to find it. More recently, researchers have attempted to bring the text and reader together by matching reader response to textual features. This moves beyond simply looking at the text but ignores many aspects of prior reader experience. In this study, the goal is to investigate how cultural discourses in which the reader is immersed, condition her construction of the text. Each reader approaches a text through the filter of both social and intellectual knowledge, deriving from her cultural world and from her own past. The challenge for researchers is to become aware of the particular levels of experience that an individual reader is applying when she responds to a text and then to discern how these organize her experience. This task is complicated by several factors. Cultural discourses by their very nature are not readily transparent. Because they represent the primary concerns within the culture, we accept many of the ideas as givens, as obvious, and are not conscious of them. We are often not aware of our assumptions and therefore do not question them until someone from a different perspective identifies them. For example, many of the readers in my study had numerous ideas about the content of romance novels without ever having read one. They often had no sense of how they had developed these ideas, stating that they had never consciously thought about them. Yet, they had absorbed them from prevailing opinions. It was only when they were confronted with reading a romance novel that they were called upon to articulate these assumptions.

Defining social discourses and how people participate in them is challenging. Any individual is part of many overlapping and competing discourses. For example, many messages in the culture may emphasize the value of romance for women. At the same time, however, women are discouraged from reading romance novels. Any reader may feel pulled in varied directions without clearly being able to define the influences at work. External opinions may act in contradictory ways—for example, many women who are comfortable about watching soap operas are contemptuous about romance novels. Themes of romance may be anathema as literature while they occupy an important role in organizing the life.

The reader is always constructing and reconstructing, affirming and reaffirming cultural discourses as she responds to the text. Although it might appear that reading is a solitary activity, it is not. The reader is always engaged in internal dialogue with the culture, asking questions like "What does it mean for me to be reading this book? What does this readership reveal about me? How do I understand it?" These questions reflect and interrogate cultural stances. Thus, the reader carries multiple ideas that are brought into play in the literary encounter.

In addition to a broad cultural influence, many readers actively seek the ideas of others, making the experience communal. They share their experiences by joining private book groups, attending book groups organized by bookstores and libraries, participating in on-line chat rooms, reading book reviews and newsletters, even influencing what gets written. Therefore, what is commonly assumed to be a private experience has many overt and covert communal properties (see Long, 1992; and Griffin, 1999 for further discussion of this point). My study of the responses of students reading romance novels explores this phenomenon by examining specific ways in which these responses evolve.

WHAT ARE ROMANCE NOVELS AND WHO READS THEM?

Romance novels provide fertile ground for this investigation. "No genre is more popular and less respected than the romance novel" (Donahue, 2002 p. 10). Such wide readership means that romance novels have entered the public discourse to such an extent that both readers and non-readers have formed opinions about them. Although there are numerous types of romances, there are certain conventions that define the genre. In the briefest description, they are relationship-driven plots with a happily-ever-after ending. "In a typical scenario, a strong-willed woman meets an equally strong-willed older man and both feel incredible antipathy—and attraction toward each other. After a series of misunderstandings, he eventually loses control of his passions and physically assaults her, but the narrative operates in such a way that this assault appears as evidence of the hero's uncontrollable love of and attraction to the heroine. Once she recognizes this in him (and he recognizes it in himself) they call a truce and declare their true—loving—feelings for one another" (Wardrop, 1995, p. 461).

In summarizing the essence of romance novels, Grant (1999) has said: "Romance literature tells us that love is the most powerful force in our lives. A story that does not convey this message is not a romance, although it may contain a romantic subplot" (p. 10). Although there are constraints to the genre, recent years have brought great diversity within the field. There is variety in terms of heroines and their professional lives, relationships of male and female characters, time periods, amount of explicit sex and so forth. The most current romances seek to replicate social norms. Thus, where heroines in earlier romances were dependent on a man for lifestyle and love, currently the heroines are often successful in their own businesses at least initially. They are independent and focused characters. In addition to the main romance plot, there is an emphasis on relationships and how these are negotiated.

Romance novels enjoy a huge readership not only in the US but also in countries throughout the world. The readership is 90% women, most of whom are lifetime readers who typically read their first romance in their teenage years and continue on through adulthood. To give an example of the prevalence of this type of fiction, in 2000, in the US, romance fiction comprised 55.9% of all paperback fiction sales; 2,289 titles were published with $1.37 billion in sales. In 1999, 41.4 million people, or 18%, of the reading-age population read a romance. One in every third woman read a romance that year.[2]

Most readers exhibit a pattern of repetitive reading, finishing one novel and rapidly moving on to another. Dedicated readers often enjoy talking with each other about the romance novels they read. Nowadays, many readers exchange and discuss views through a large array of computer sites. They may use the internet for discussions with authors, as well as provide book reviews, relevant interviews and so forth.

Despite the popularity of romance novels, the culture at large harbors a deep suspicion toward romances that has led to their marginal position.

Few people realize how much courage it takes for a woman to open a romance on an airplane. She knows what everyone around her will think both about her and her choice of reading material. When it comes to romance novels, society has always felt free to sit in judgment not only on the literature but on the reader herself. (Krentz, 1992, p. 1)

There are several reasons for this. As fiction, both written by and for women, romance novels "have been stigmatized by the low status of their female readers and writers" (Jensen, 1984, p. 23). There may, in fact, be a deep-seated dislike for and prejudice against a genre that appeals almost exclusively to women. Proponents of such views may be suspicious of a

---

[2] These statistics were compiled by the Book Industry Study Group (2000).

form of literature that appears to give so much pleasure to women. Others
may spurn the books because they believe they are of poor quality. For example, Mosley, Charles & Havir (1995) have compiled a list of reasons why
librarians have been reluctant to stock romances. A sampling is as follows:
1) Romances are formula books; 2) Smart people do not read romances; 3)
Romances are too sexually explicit; 4) Romances are not good books, they
are trash; 5) The covers are too steamy; 6) All romances are alike—If you've
read one, you've read them all.

Previously hostile to romances but recently reformed, Mosley and
other librarians are puzzled by the strength of the criticisms leveled at
the romance novels. Most of these criticisms could as easily be applied to
other types of books that appear in libraries without benefit of controversy.
For example, popular mysteries could be labeled as equally formulaic. Although some romances have explicit sex, many have far less than other
popular best sellers. Mosley and her co-authors pose questions about the
imposition of these cultural standards. They wonder who is to decide what
literature is lowbrow and highbrow and even whether such decisions need
to be made. They point out that Dickens wrote serialized fiction for the
popular press that has crossed the line from lowbrow to highbrow. This
awareness of shifting values reveals the ways in which attitudes change
as the culture changes. It is worth thinking about what these attitudes
mean. How do certain books and types of literature acquire cultural authority while this is denied to others? What is the role of the librarian? Is
it to set and reinforce standards or to provide what readers want? What
happens to the reader when these types of standards are imposed? Are
books harmful to readers? Can multiple standards co-exist or will some
readers come to feel that they have made inferior choices and thus feel
marginalized?

Scholarly interest in the legitimacy of the romance novel received a
big stimulus from the 1984 publication of *Reading the Romance* by Janice
Radway. Her research followed a new approach, focusing on the reading
experiences of a group of dedicated readers. Previous analyses of the romance reading experience had not been based on the reactions of these
habitual readers. Her group of readers found the books and the reading
of them to be extremely positive in their lives. They saw themselves as
educating themselves through the history, diverse locales and vocabulary
in the books. They believed the fact that they had chosen reading as their
leisure time activity was positively coded in our society. At the same time,
these readers described the escape value of the romance: emotionally, this
reading provided escape from the rigors of caring for others. Radway was
interested in what aspects of the content appealed to readers. In analyzing the plots, she found an interesting phenomenon. While the men were

described as spectacularly masculine and often gruff, they become very loving and nurturing by the end of the book. Building on the research of Chodorow (1978), she noted that women often become depleted by their role as caretakers of their families and long for someone to nurture and look after them. Romances offer a vicarious experience for women longing to be cared for. By identifying with the development of the love relationship, the reader can experience a man who becomes very tender and loving. It was very important to Radway's readers that the books follow this pattern. Readers often checked the conclusion before purchasing a novel to insure an ending that satisfied this desire. Once this content was confirmed, readers nurtured themselves in another way—they created a time and setting for the reading that removed them from normal concerns and enabled them to carve out time and space for themselves. Many readers described the luxury of being alone and absorbed as an important component of the process.

However, two less positive results of romance reading should also be noted. First, the reader may derive enough satisfaction from the reading and accompanying fantasies to permit her to stay in what may not be a good or satisfying situation. Second, she may be led to believe that change in her own relationship is just as possible as it appeared to be in the novel. Radway (1984) describes how transformations of the hero are illusory and do not depict a mature change arising from growth in relationship capacity.

Radway focused on novels published by Harlequin during the 1970s. Thurston (1987), writing a few years later, emphasized the messages in later novels. She believed that the romance novels that achieved greater popularity as the decade of the 80s unfolded were responsive to the cultural changes brought about by feminism and the sexual revolution. Not only was there more explicit sex, but the heroines were more dynamic women who had career ambitions and were assertive in their lives and relationships. Thurston believed that these novels gave women positive role models. More recent scholars (see, for example, Krentz, 1992, Kaler, 1999) have also emphasized the liberating aspects of the romance novel. For example the argument is made that it is important for the romance reader to see a heroine who is making choices and functioning in the world: "In today's romance fiction, women win" (Charles, Mosley & Boricus, 1999). These scholars believe that heroines can function as role models showing the way to independence and self-reliance. The more recent, feisty heroines know what they want and get it. No longer are they in need of a man for survival and required to be submissive in order to secure him. On the other hand, some (e.g., Wagner, 1995) see these heroines as subversive. While the rest of the culture is male-centered, these books star a strong woman character.

From a different perspective, some feminists have expressed concern about the messages contained in romance novels, which they believe are anathema to the interests of women. These critics believe that the heavy emphasis on relationship as a way of solving problems, status inequities, gender stereotypes and so forth will serve to reaffirm women's secondary position in society rather than challenging them to act for change.

Even following a brief review of the literature, one can see that there are conflicting ideas about how romances are embedded in our culture. While it is clear that exposure to them is extensive, it is unclear what they mean to those who read them.

The popularity of romance novels has recently spawned a burgeoning academic interest in both the messages within and the impact of romance novels. Scholars concerned with women's perspectives have been particularly interested in examining the impact of popular culture on lived experience. They have examined the effects of reading romance novels by examining how the novels affect women's lives and how adequately they represent women's experiences in our culture. In other words, in what ways are they prescriptive and in what ways descriptive?

USE IN THE CLASSROOM

As an adjunct to this growing academic interest, reading and analyzing romance novels has become a popular activity in the women's studies classroom. (Crawford, 1994; Ricker-Wilson, 1999) Although previously considered alien to the academic environment, romance novels are currently seen as providing an entry into an important aspect of popular culture. Understanding their popularity, impact, and content, tells us something about the experience of a large number of women. Feminist scholars, in particular, have utilized textual analysis of romance novels to demonstrate patterns of female/male relationships in our society. Allied to this is an interest in the meanings and influences of popular culture.

During the last several years, I have taught a course, *Women and Psychology*, in which students have been assigned to read romance novels. After reading a novel which they have selected, students write papers in which they describe: 1) their initial feelings about romance novels; 2) their analyses of the relationships and societal images portrayed in the texts; and 3) their understandings of the reasons for and impact of repeated readings of the texts. These guidelines are there to stimulate them to explore their prior assumptions about, as well as their actual responses to, the experience of reading the romance novel. After they have completed this assignment and had time to reflect on their own reactions, there is an extensive class discussion that gives students the opportunity to reflect upon and analyze the nature of their own responses, as well as to consider the similarities and differences of their respective reading experiences.

In general, my students indicated that they had either limited or no previous exposure to romance novels. However, as a result of powerful, widely-held cultural attitudes, they inevitably approached the task of reading a romance novel deeply influenced by prevalent social discourses. These discourses guide the way in which they think and feel about the assignment—starting with the practical issue of being seen purchasing the book to the way they react to the book's content.

I want now to elaborate further the ways in which popular discourses enter into the entire process: the social anxieties surrounding the romance novel as well as the reactions to the text itself. All the student readers approached the situation with multiple expectations, which reflect wider popular discourses. Nearly all students had a wealth of ideas whose genesis one student described as "the greater culture has played a role in forming my opinion." In other words, they had absorbed a series of ideas without particular awareness of them until this activity called them into play.

RESPONSES

Analyses of student papers in my class produced over the last several years, demonstrate how students react to the concept of reading a romance novel, how they approach the task, and what their responses are to the texts themselves. Early on, it became apparent that it was necessary to try and unfold the layers of assumptions that guided readers from the inception of the assignment. As soon as students became aware of what lay before them, their conceptions of the meaning of the task came into play. I try to capture the responses as students are told about the assignment, what it is like for them to go into a store and be identified as a reader of romance novels, and how comfortable they are with friends and family knowing they are reading a romance. It is in these acts and the behaviors that accompany them that they are able to identify and label their own assumptions. The responses fall into several distinguishable categories that reveal how students view the books, their evaluation of the readers of romances, and the status of romances within the culture.

The readers described here are both graduate and undergraduate students in *Women and Psychology* seminars at a small Catholic liberal arts college for women. For most, this was an initial exposure to women's studies and thus the first time they were called on to think about the status of women in the culture. They found the assignment of reading a romance novel surprising. In general they were embarrassed that, as college students, they would be seen reading what they considered inferior literature. Some described family taboos based on the supposition that the books mainly involved sexual relations. Most reported that they had simply not wanted to read the books in the past, although in some cases family members were known to read them.

Before actually reading a romance, these students clearly had a set of ideas which colored their experience. Listed below are underlying assumptions derived from student responses regarding the readers of the text as well as the content and literary value.

I. *Assumptions*

Assumptions regarding the genre derive, in most cases, from larger social discourse concerned with what the books are, who reads them, and the role they play in the culture.

1. *Assumptions about the readers of romance novels.*
1. a. **Readers lack romantic relationships.**

   • *Nearly everyone that I spoke to about reading the book made comments about lonely or desperate women reading romances.*

1. b. **Readers lack sexual relationships.**

   • *Romance novels seem to focus on physical beauty and the intensity of lust. Maybe this is a stimulating topic for some women who perhaps are looking for a more exciting, lust-filled sex life.*

2. *Assumptions about literary level.* This category of response was the evaluations of the books themselves: beliefs that the books are formulaic and without literary merit.
2. a. **Romance novels are of poor quality: minimal character and plot development.**

   • *I've never considered them to be worthwhile reading material and therefore never took the time to read one.*

2. b. **Romance novels are oriented around excessive "trashy" sex.**

   • *As far as my opinion on romance novels, well, I believed that they usually lack a good plot, contain way too much sex, and are in general rather boring.*
   • *Moreover, prior to reading the book I really did not have any respect for romance novels. I thought they would be a total waste of time and equated romance novels with trashy pornographic texts made for women.*

3. *Assumptions about feminist/anti-feminist messages.* This category is concerned with the assumed content of romance novels. Readers anticipate negative portrayals of women as dependent and in need of a man.

3. a. **Women will be portrayed as weak and passive.**

- *Before I read my romance novel, I already had preconceived notions about romance novels. I thought they were cheesy, corny and portrayed women as weaklings and submissive to men.*
- *Furthermore, I thought that women's and men's sex roles would be portrayed in very traditional terms. For instance, the man would be constantly "rescuing" the woman, who would be viewed as not being able to take care of herself.*
- *This stems from my preconceived notion that these books would be filled with negative depictions of women.*

3. b. **Romantic relationships will be unreal.**

- *My opinion of romance novels is that they are predictable in their portrayal of an idealized and immature view of love. They perpetuate the stereotype of a powerless damsel who is rescued by the so-called love of a strong Casanova.*

Because of what readers assumed they would find in romance novels and from their stereotypes of the readers, they anticipated what their own encounters would be. As a result, they were embarrassed to purchase the books and to be seen reading them. They anticipated a stigma attached to romance novels that would label them as deficient. They thought that reading these books detracted from their scholarly standing. They therefore covered the books when reading them in public and were careful to assure others that this reading had been imposed on them by a professor, not selected by them. Assumptions about the novels provided an elaborated set of expectations of what they would find and what their experience would be.

II. *Anticipations*

The assumptions led readers to anticipate their own experience.

1. *Anticipations about content*
1a. **Readers predict that they will be offended by finding too much sexual content.**

- *Before reading the book I felt kind of confused because I thought romance novels are trashy and are filled with sex, so what is there to learn from them or analyze about them?*

1.b. **Readers anticipate boredom because of low literary quality.**

- *When I was first assigned this project I was not really excited because I thought these books would have no story line and would not hold my interest.*
- *I approached this assignment with something like dread. I thought it would be boring, trivial and irrelevant to counseling. For me the romance novel is devoid of plot or character development.*

1. c. **Readers anticipate that the books will be entertaining.**

- *I was excited about the assignment because I knew it would be easy reading and people were saying that you get hooked on the story, so I was curious to find out.*

2. *Anticipations about the reactions of others.*

2. a. **Readers fear they will be assumed to possess all of the negative characteristics they believe are connected with the books and their readers.**

- *It occurred to me that I was embarrassed to be seen reading the book because I think that the type of people who read this type of book are generally lonely, depressed people looking for love and adventure in their lives.*

2. b. **Readers express curiosity about how to account for the popularity of romance novels.**

- *I approached this assignment with mixed emotions. On the one hand, the idea of actually reading this kind of novel attracted me because I must admit that I was always somewhat curious to see what appeal they held; what it was that kept people reading them.*

For a small number of students, these assumptions and anticipations were borne out. Their attitudes remained unaltered throughout their contact with the novels. However, a larger number were surprised that their interest was captured by the romances. They did not anticipate that they would forsake other interests, including sleep, as they became immersed in the book. What changed for these readers? It seems that another compelling social force intervened: the value of romance. Although uncomfortable with the idea of romance novels, they were attracted by the romance itself. This attraction resonated for them and engaged them far more than they had anticipated. Some examples of how response to romance affected readers follow.

III. *The Value of Romance*

The idea of value presents romance as an important and organizing goal in a woman's life—a view that finds expression in the novels. This relates to the discourse of desire that has been widely documented.

- *I think the appeal of these books is something that has been rooted in women from the time they are just little girls. They are basically the same fairy tales that we all grew up with, only now we are getting them in the adult version. These books allow us to continue on the fantasies that we not only had as children but were encouraged to have.*
- *In the beginning I actually had to force myself to read it. Then it happened. It started to get good. There was passion and heat.*
- *These books play a significant role in the readers' lives because the books allow the readers to escape into a fantasy world where their unfulfilled dreams can be filled.*

ROMANCE IN OUR CULTURE

I now want to explore the ideas surrounding the cultural portrayal of romance—the ways in which romance is represented in our culture and how ideas about romance influence developing girls.

Several bodies of literature approach the ways in which romance is promoted as central to the lives of women. Although girls do not generally start reading romances until the teen years, there are many precursors that have laid the foundation for this interest. Romance reading forms a continuous line with the other types of media experiences that girls have had from early childhood. From a very early age, through toys, literature, magazines, television, and movies, girls are given the strong message that what is ultimately important for them is their ability to attract a male. Although this might seem an outdated idea in this time of feminist consciousness, a review of various literatures shows the strength of this age-old concept. Despite the fact that women have made gains in the professional world, they have been unable to displace the central role of romance in their lives. Perhaps this is because the messages start at a very young age and are pervasive as they grow up.

One of the earliest literatures with which they have contact, fairy tales, promotes the fantasy of beautiful girls who will be rescued by the prince. Although in recent years a counter tradition of fairy tales has been developed in which the girls are heroic and refuse simply to accept the prince, these new tales are still only accessible to a limited audience. Romance novels are frequently portrayed as fairy tales for women. While distinguishing the two, Smith (1999) emphasized the similarity of themes in both genres: This is a just world where the good are rewarded.

Regarding the process of girls' maturation, there is a whole literature that takes up this theme in a variety of ways. For example, many girls read teen magazines. Readership starts at the preteen stage. Although some of these have names like Young Modern, they continue, largely, to convey the messages that a girl/woman finds fulfillment in a man. There are many magazines aimed first at the teenage audience and later at more mature women. Although these offer helpful messages to the woman about how to manage her career, there continues to be a heavy focus on a girl's/woman's sex appeal and instruction in how to attract a man. Analyses of the fictional literature (Pierce, 1993) in teen magazines found they continue to present girls with stereotypic messages. The conflicts which the girl encounters in these stories usually revolve around boys. The girl is typically unable to resolve her conflicts, and depends on outside sources to do so. In other words, girls need others to help solve their problems. They are reinforced in the idea that their importance derives from their relationships with men. Christian-Smith (1993) showed how this same theme reverberates in series books like *The Babysitter's Club* that are targeted to young girls and promoted by scholastic book clubs.

The strength of the romance orientation is demonstrated in the oft-quoted work by Holland and Eisenhart, *Educated in Romance* (1990). Interested in the question of why so few women pursued careers in math and science, these authors did a longitudinal study in which they followed young women at two universities. These were women who entered college with strong high school records and high aspirations for academic achievement and professional careers. About half planned careers in math or science. What did they find? Less than a third of these women fulfilled these expectations. "Most had ended up with intense involvements in heterosexual romantic relationships, marginalized career identities, and inferior preparation for their likely roles as breadwinners...They seem to have willingly scaled down their aspirations for careers and entered into marriage in economic positions inferior to those of their husbands" (pp. 4–5). What these researchers emphasize is that no system of overt and institutionalized discrimination forced these women into these behaviors. Instead, the cultural values pressured women into believing that their true goal was success on the "sexual auction block". For women, negotiating their sexual attractiveness within the social system at the college was of prime importance. Although this was also important for male students, it was one of a number of attributes that contributed to their overall evaluation by the peer culture.

It is clear that women are raised to believe that romance is central to their lives. This applies to all women, including those in the academy. No women in our culture are immune to this demand. So when women encounter romance novels, the resonance is there. When she reads the romance novel, a woman is given the opportunity to replay over and over the crucial moment in her life when she was desired and sought after. Heilbrun (1988) described this moment in the following way: "For a short time during courtship, the illusion is maintained that women, by withholding themselves, are central. Women are allowed this brief period in the limelight—and it is the part of their lives most constantly and vividly enacted in a myriad of representations. . . ." (p. 21). As Heilbrun pointed out, it is this stage where the woman is the center of attention. Once she is captured, there is no longer the need to seduce her. The romance novel replays this central moment over and over again. Frequently the book ends at the moment the characters decide to join their lives.

The ways in which the ideas of romance are promulgated in society are highly seductive to women. Thus, at least on the surface level, romance novels have the capacity to resonate with fantasies and expectations that have been inculcated from an early age. Over and over, then, the woman romance reader can identify with a heroine who is selected and valued for her qualities.

If, wherever they turn in the popular culture, girls and women are reaffirmed in the idea that romance is the dominant and most crucial quest in their lives, it makes sense that they enjoy reliving and/or fantasizing this quest repeatedly. Again and again, while reading the romance novel, a woman participates in a successful romantic outcome. She can identify with the hazards of the quest knowing that the woman and man will be happily united in the end. Radway (1984) found that her readers often checked the conclusion of the book before purchase so they could ensure that it would give them the story they wished for. The formulaic quality of the books, for which they are so heavily criticized, rather than representing a negative quality, can be seen as positive. It ensures that the key themes are available to the reader over and over; only the details need to change, the nature of the quest can acceptably replay itself. As Heilbrun (1988) noted, the moment of courtship is central to a woman's life.[3] When reading a romance novel, she can replay the feelings from that time—or those she can imagine would be there. So, with ideas of the value of romance firmly entrenched, the reader is receptive to its flow in the romance novel. However, these ideas both exist alongside and conflict with the assumptions and anticipations she

---

[3] While this study refers to novels based on heterosexual relationships, an important comparison would be with lesbian romance novels.

brought with her to the experience. Few readers easily allied themselves with a single stance. Most found themselves balancing a variety of positions throughout the response process.

SUMMARY AND CONCLUSIONS

When we look at the process of constructing meaning in response to a text, we are interested in what the reader brings to the text and what the text brings to the reader. Both elements are necessary to understand the engagement and the meaning that is produced. Many analyses have focused on textual structure and content and how these features elicit response from the reader. Although, the importance of what the reader brings to the encounter has been acknowledged, the substance of her experience and its impact has been difficult to ascertain. I have approached this aspect through an examination of the cultural dialogues with which the reader is acquainted and have explored how these influence her responses.

For the majority of the student readers, various conflicting discourses were engaged during the process of reading. To a large extent, the students had accepted a general social perspective that romance novels are a negative influence and had extended this prejudicial evaluation to the people who read them. Such attitudes had inhibited these students in the past and continued to influence them as they read the romance for the assignment. Their negative *a priori* evaluation affected the preliminary activities of purchasing the book, which requires public association with romance novels. These students felt a pervasive distaste toward the whole endeavor; but among them were also some who were simultaneously curious and willing to undertake the task. While the anticipation was largely negative, the experience was not. Many students came into class describing their surprise at being captured by the books and staying up late into the night reading. They had not anticipated the attraction. Many were also surprised by the content, finding the heroines more dynamic and sexual activity a far less dominant role than expected. These readers subsequently worked to reconcile their preconceptions with their experience. Some resolved the contradictions by deciding that despite the fact that they enjoyed the novel they would not be likely to read another.

No reader stood outside of her experience within the culture. Aware of it or not, responses were always in relation to the culture. Students constructed meaning within these cultural constraints. Different cultural discourses may be appropriate to a particular reader's experience and may present a conflict. Students moved among competing discourses by balancing them, revising some, rethinking others. Awareness of this process facilitates our understanding of how readers respond to texts.

REFERENCES

Book Industry Study Group. (2000). *http://www*. Rwanational.org/statistics.stm.

Charles, John, Mosley, Shelley, & Bouricus, Ann. (1999). Romancing the young adult reader. *Voice of Youth Advocates, 21*, 6: 414–19.

Chodorow, N. (1978). *The reproduction of mothering: Psychoanalysis and the sociology of gender*. Berkeley, CA: University of California Press.

Christian-Smith, Linda K. (Ed.). (1993). *Texts of desire: Essays on fiction, femininity and schooling*. London: The Falmer Press.

Crawford, Mary. (1994). Rethinking the romance: Teaching the content and function of gender stereotypes in the *Psychology of Women* course. *Teaching of Psychology, 21*, 3, 151–153

Donahue, Deidre. (2002). "The look of love is in your eyes." *USA Today*, Feb. 7.

Grant, Vanessa. (1999). Secrets of romantic conflict. *The Writer, 112*, 5, 10–12.

Griffin, Linda. (1999). An analysis of meaning creation through the integration of sociology and literature: A critical ethnography of a romance reading group. A dissertation presented to the faculties of the University of Houston and Rice University.

Gruber, Howard E. (1989). The evolving systems approach to creative work. In Doris B. Wallace & Howard E. Gruber (Eds.), *Creative people at work: Twelve cognitive case studies*. New York: Oxford University Press.

Gruber, Howard E. (1994). The social construction of extraordinary selves: Collaboration among unique creative people. Paper presented at the Fourth Annual Esther Katz Symposium on the Psychological Development of Gifted Children: Developing General vs. Specific Abilities and their Relationship to Diversity. The University of Kansas, Lawrence, Kansas.

Heilbrun, C. (1988). *Writing a woman's life*. New York: Ballantine Books.

Holland, Dorothy C., & Eisenhart, Margaret A. (1990). *Educated in romance*. Chicago: University of Chicago Press.

Jensen, Margaret Ann. (1984). *Loves $weet return: The Harlequin story*. Bowling Green, Ohio: Bowling Green State University Popular Press.

Kaler, Anne K. & Johnson-Kurek, Rosemary (Eds.). (1999). *Romantic conventions*. Bowling Green, Ohio: Bowling Green State University Popular Press.

Krentz, Jayne Anne (Ed). (1992). *Dangerous men and adventurous women*. Philadelphia: University of Pennsylvania Press.

Mosley, Shelley, Charles, John, and Havir, Julie. (May, 1995). The librarian as effete snob: Why romance? *Wilson Library Bulletin, 69*, pp. 24–25.

Long, Elizabeth. (1992). Textual interpretation as collective action. *Discourse, 14*, 3: 104–30.

Pierce, Kate. (1993). Socialization of teenage girls through teen-magazine fiction: the making of a new woman or an old lady? *Sex Roles, 29*, 1/2. 59–68.

Radway, Janice. (1984). *Reading the romance*. Chapel Hill: University of North Carolina Press.

Ricker-Wilson, Carol. (1999). Busting textual bodices: Gender, reading, and the popular romance. *English Journal, 88*, 3. pp. 57–64.

Smith, Jennifer Crusie. (1999). This is not your mother's Cinderella: The romance novel as feminist fairy tale. In Kaler, Anne K., & Johnson-Kurek, Rosemary (Eds.), *Romantic conventions*. Bowling Green, Ohio: Bowling Green State University Popular Press.

Thurston, Carol. (1987). *The romance revolution*. Chicago: University of Illinois Press.

Wagner, Betst. (1995). Living the fantasy. *US News and World Report, 119*: 78–81.

Wardrop, Stephanie. (Fall 1995). The heroine is being beaten: Freud, sadomasochism, and reading the romance. *Style, 29*, pp. 459–73.

4

THE ROLE OF SOCIAL COMPARISON IN THE ARTISTIC DEVELOPMENT OF VINCENT VAN GOGH

Richard Brower

The Other as the synthetic unity of his experiences and as both will and passion comes to organize my experiences.

Jean-Paul Sartre ("Being and Nothingness")

INTRODUCTION

July 29, 1990, the television newscaster Charles Kuralt, discussing the idea of an artists' colony, asked what the purpose was of an artists' colony since artists are so isolated. Mr. Kuralt went on to describe Vincent van Gogh as "that great loner." Mr. Kuralt's statement is representative of an unexamined popular belief that mystifies creative work and depicts the creative person as basically solitary and working in solitude. In general, this picture is quite inaccurate. As far as van Gogh is concerned, he may have been difficult to get along with; he may have been argumentative; and may have developed an individual philosophy and a unique style which was not understood nor appreciated very much in his lifetime. But he was not a loner. He was certainly lonely from time to time; but he never avoided other people. During every period of his development as a person and an artist, he maintained a network of social relations pertinent to his work. While in Paris, for example (1886–1888), this network included Paul Gauguin, Paul Signac, Henri de Toulouse-Lautrec, Charles Verlat, and Georges Seurat, among others. Van Gogh was especially skilled at learning from others. He was able to incorporate the work of others while at the same time establishing his own independent style.

In this chapter, I make use of social comparison theory as a viable way of understanding important aspects of creative work. I focus on its role in the artistic, intellectual and spiritual growth of an individual creator, the Dutch artist Vincent van Gogh. Social comparison theory, first proposed by Leon Festinger (1954), has developed considerably in the five decades since Festinger and has recently been represented in a comprehensive handbook of theory and research (Suls & Wheeler, 2000). The theory maintains that comparisons with others may play a significant role in a person's self-evaluation and subjective well-being (Buunk & Gibbons, 1997). At the individual level, such comparisons result in a reorganization of thought and affect and, thus, in a new meaning of the evolving self-image. Motives for comparison include cognitive processes, such as seeking information, as well as emotional issues of self esteem (Wayment & Taylor, 1995), and self-enhancement (Wills, 1981) Three types of social comparison proposed in the theory are pertinent to an understanding of the relationship between a person's creativity and his or her social comparisons: (1) *upward social comparison*, i.e. comparing oneself with someone judged to be better than oneself; (2) *downward social comparison*, i.e. comparing oneself with someone judged to be not as good as oneself; and (3) *lateral social comparison*, i.e. comparison with another who is more or less equal.

My study of Vincent van Gogh has been influenced by the *Evolving Systems Approach* developed by Howard Gruber (see Gruber, 1981, Gruber & Davis, 1988, Wallace & Gruber, 1989). Using intense and detailed case study examination, Gruber and his colleagues attempted to understand how an indisputably creative person actually does his or her work. The approach requires that the investigator pay close attention to the person's organization of three loosely coupled systems: knowledge, purpose, and affect; and by carefully detailing the person's thought and work over time, to understand how that particular creator produced a novel idea, theory, and product. Gruber has developed the methodologies and techniques to enable the investigator to fulfill these requirements (see, for example, Gruber & Davis, 1988). At the heart of Gruber's theory is the idea that the creator is an intensely focused person, often engaged in the pursuit of an overarching idea which, in turn, spawns a "network" of multiple enterprises—some sequential, some simultaneous. In *Darwin on Man* (1981), his case study of Charles Darwin, Gruber demonstrated that creativity demands purposeful, protracted work, which can include dozens, perhaps hundreds, of insights, leading metaphors, and other significant tropes. Creativity does not consist of a single spectacular insight and other mysterious and unknowable processes.

In this chapter, I examine the life and work of Vincent van Gogh and consider one system that figured prominently in the development of his creative skills—his network of social and professional encounters and their influence on his development as a creative artist.

In order to undertake such a study, it is essential, of course, that sufficient material and original sources are available.

LETTERS

Van Gogh's letters represent an extraordinary and revealing body of information. Van Gogh wrote letters copiously. Most were to his brother Theo, who retained the great majority. Unfortunately, Vincent did not keep his brother's letters to him so the available correspondence is essentially one way. One of the reasons van Gogh's letters are so powerful is because they are pure "thinking aloud" material. He carried paper with him and jotted down his thoughts while he was creating. His writings are therefore not distorted by the passage of time and the haziness of memory that attends it. Van Gogh also wrote many letters to his friends and collaborators. The letters give a firm picture of his thinking during critical phases of his creative work. They also supply us with a profile of the shifting quality of his moods, and emotions concerning significant events, people, places and activities. The letters to Theo are vivid, detailed, and often moving.

In his letters, van Gogh also reveals the gentleness, love of humanity and clarity of thought about his art that he maintained throughout his working life—qualities that have been neglected in the sensationalized accounts of his brief psychotic episodes.

CHILDHOOD

On March 30, 1852 in the village of Groot Zundert, Holland, Anna Cornelia Carbentus van Gogh, 33 years old, gave birth to her first child. It was a still-born son. Christened Vincent Willem van Gogh, he was buried in the cemetery of the local church. Exactly one year later, also on March 30, in 1853, Anna Cornelia gave birth to a healthy son and he too was named

Vincent. As a young boy, walking to school or church, past the fresh-cut grass and the neat rows of tombstones, Vincent van Gogh must have had food for thought at seeing a tombstone bearing his own name and birth date of March 30. There was a dead Vincent van Gogh, his brother, and a living one, himself.

Vincent's parents were loving and attentive. His father, Theodorus van Gogh, born 1822, was a Protestant pastor in the village of Groot Zundert, which was in southern Holland, near the Belgian border. He was known as "the handsome parson" and considered by people who knew him as an amiable, straight-forward man. Vincent's mother, Anna Carbentus, was the daughter of a bookseller, and considered by people who knew her as a kind, considerate, respected person.

Van Gogh came from a relatively unremarkable background. His ancestors had been art dealers, consuls, goldsmiths, preachers, and there had been a sculptor. There were no direct precursors for the kind of talent revealed by Vincent.

After Vincent, Anna and Theodorus had five more children. These were Anna Cornelia, Theodorus (Theo), four years younger than Vincent, Elizabeth Huberta, Cornelis Vincent, and Wilhelmina Jacoba (Wil). During his adult years, Vincent remained close to Wilhelmina, his youngest sister, and extremely close to his brother, and staunch supporter, Theo. The collaboration between Theo and Vincent remains one of the most remarkable in the history of art; it is difficult to imagine Vincent's creative work without the support of, and feedback from, his younger brother.

Johanna Bonger, Theo's wife, reported that, as a child, Vincent had a difficult temper, was often troublesome and strong-willed. She noted his great love for animals and flowers, and his delight in collecting things; but there was no indication, during his childhood, that Vincent had unusual artistic talent.

ART DEALER'S APPRENTICE

Vincent's Uncle Cent (also named Vincent) was a successful art dealer. In 1858, he was offered a partnership in the prominent firm of Goupil and Co., in Paris. He subsequently opened a branch of the firm in The Hague, Holland, where he got young Vincent, then sixteen, an apprenticeship as an art dealer. The Hague branch of Goupil was headed by Herman Tersteeg, who became quite an important figure in van Gogh's life, though their relationship was difficult and van Gogh was very conflicted in his views of Tersteeg. Tersteeg was important and influential in the art world and later also bought one of van Gogh's drawings. But van Gogh was extremely critical of Tersteeg, who was a pragmatic person, and had somewhat conventional and commercially-slanted views about what and how an artist should paint. At Goupil, Vincent was exposed to a variety of art, and, under supervision, assisted in the sale of paintings, photographs, engravings, lithographs, and reproductions. Vincent worked as an apprentice until he was 23, when he was fired for conducting himself inappropriately. According to his superiors he would commonly and inappropriately discuss the merits of the works of art with customers and frequently talk them out of sales. At Goupil, van Gogh learned much about art and began to develop his own moral, political, and artistic values about what was good, what was worthwhile, and what pandered to the lowest common denominator of public taste.

After this experience, Vincent tried various jobs, including teacher, book dealer, and lay minister. Until he was 27, in 1880, he tried out these activities in the search of a meaningful career. While he was working as an enthusiastic book dealer in Dordrecht, Holland, a fellow lodger wrote of him:

> He was a singular man with a singular appearance into the bargain. He was well made, and had reddish hair which stood up on end; his face was homely and covered with freckles, but changed and brightened wonderfully when he warmed into enthusiasm, which happened often enough. Van Gogh proved laughter repeatedly by his attitude and behavior—for everything he did and thought and felt, and his way of living, was different from that of others of his age" (Treble, 1975, p. 11).

In May 1877 van Gogh left Dordrecht and went north to Amsterdam. He had decided he wanted to study theology, an idea he had been thinking about for some time. In Dordrecht he began to prepare for the state exam that would allow him to do so. He also set out to improve himself. Realizing that he was impulsive, he recognized that he needed to exercise patience and discipline, and wrote to his brother Theo:

> I have a lot of work to do and it is not very easy, but patience will help me through. I hope to remember the ivy 'which stealth on though he wears no wings'; as the ivy creeps along the walls, so the pen must crawl over the paper (NYGS, Letter 95, 19 May 1877).[1]

He was referring to the writing he was required to do to prepare for his theological studies. In this same letter, he commented that there were certain features that religion and painting had in common, such as a step-by-step process, and the considerable study time that both demanded. He told Theo about some cheap prints he had bought to hang up in his

---

[1] For van Gogh's letters, I have used the New York Graphics Society (1978) collection, henceforth referred to as NYGS; and Stone (1978).

room, his descriptions of them clearly revealing his love of art. He enclosed an engraving on a religious subject as a gift to Theo—thus expressing his love for his brother as well as his religious passion.

DECISION TO BE AN ARTIST

In 1878, van Gogh secured a position as a lay minister in a coal-mining village in Belgium, in an area called the Borinage, having decided not to pursue his formal religious studies, which would have taken another seven years. As was his custom, he threw himself into his work, giving away his belongings, living on bread and water, and taking sick miners into his own home. He also began sketching the miners.

From the beginning he had admired and respected these members of his congregation and seemed to identify with them. He described them in a letter to Theo:

> they are intelligent and quick at their difficult work; brave and frank...they are short but square-shouldered, with melancholy deep-set eyes. They are skillful at many things, and work terribly hard. They have a nervous temperament—I do not mean weak, but very sensitive. They have an innate, deep-rooted hatred and a strong mistrust of anyone who is domineering. With miners one must have a miner's character and temperament, and no pretentious pride or mastery, or one will never get along with them or gain their confidence. (NYGS, Letter 129, April 1879).

Van Gogh's relationship with his church superiors was strained. They were dismayed that he would not follow rules. Taking sick miners to his home to try to nurse them back to health was against church policy. Friction increased. Reprimands for his excessive zeal with the miners went unheeded. Finally, in July of 1879, he was told that his appointment would not be extended. Van Gogh moved to a neighboring village where he read a great deal and pursued his interest in drawing. He was, once again, questioning the direction of his life's work. He went home for some time to visit his parents, in spite of the bad feelings between him and his father. The latter had been shocked and bitterly disappointed that Vincent had decided not to pursue the formal study of theology and that his vocation would not be passed on. He also disapproved of his son's apparent indifference to earning money to support himself. After some months of soul searching, van Gogh decided, in the summer of 1879, to return to the Borinage. In a letter to Theo, he wrote of his chosen path in characteristically moral terms—he believed an artist's vocation was sublime and admirable.

STARTING OUT

Vincent van Gogh was born in 1853 and died in 1890, at the age of 37. Although he had done many sketches and drawings from an early age, he was a full-time artist for only ten years—the last ten years of his life. His ten-year career as an artist started out by anchoring to several things. He sought the tutelage of his renowned cousin Anton Mauve. He chose heroes from the art world he wanted to emulate, including Millet and Rembrandt. He resolved to become competent in drawing before proceeding to painting. He decided to find some way to infuse his art with action and emotion.

By the autumn of 1880, he had done what he could by himself. He had read assiduously on perspective and anatomy and studied drawing from borrowed books. He copied from the etchings and prints of other artists which he had bought earlier or from ones sent to him by Theo. Of course, he now had no income and no money to pay rent, never mind buying the materials—paper etc.—to do his work. Theo gave him financial support and sent him supplies, and Vincent, as ever, lived only on the barest necessities, even more frugally than when he was a lay preacher. But he knew he had finally found his true profession and his trajectory. In September, 1880, he wrote Theo:

> I cannot tell you how happy I am that I have taken up drawing again. I had been thinking about it for a long time, but always considered it impossible & beyond my capabilities. But now, though I continue to be conscious of my failings & of my depressing dependence on a great many things, now I have recovered my peace of mind & my energy increases by the day...For me the object is to learn to draw well, to gain control of my pencil, my charcoal or my brush. Once I have achieved that I shall be able to do good work almost anywhere and the Borinage is as picturesque as old Venice, as Arabia or Brittany, Normandy. (NYGS, Letter 136, 24 September, 1880.)

Van Gogh always needed to find the support of other artists and not just those of his own generation. He greatly respected the opinion of Anton Mauve who was a leading artist in his day, as well as a cousin by marriage. He contacted Mauve and arranged for art lessons in The Hague. Van Gogh learned drawing and water coloring from Mauve. In a letter to Theo, he described his dedication to this work:

> Drawing becomes more and more a passion with me, and it is a passion just like that of a sailor for the sea. Mauve has now shown me a new way to make something, that is, how to paint water colours. Well, I am quite absorbed in this now and sit daubing and washing out again; in short, I am trying to find a way. (NYGS. Letter 170, 7 January, 1882.)

Van Gogh also realized the limitations of following the dictates of a single other artist and he explained to Theo that, while he was fond of Mauve and liked his work very much, he did not want to confine himself to the school that Mauve represented, or any one school for that matter. Throughout his development, van Gogh copied, translated and used the works of others as the basis for formulating his own style. In 1880 he had written that he believed copying good art was a good foundation for an artist's work.

Mauve was important to van Gogh in many ways. He helped him financially to set up a studio in The Hague. He taught him how to draw and showed him the treatment of diverse media, including crayons and water color. He oriented van Gogh to the Barbizon school, a group of painters who emphasized earth colors and an interest in working with peasants as subject matter.

In the first years of his artistic work, devoted to drawing, van Gogh often included his drawings in his letters to Theo, commenting on them and critiquing them. He was very well read and had already studied da Vinci's *Notebooks* (Richter, 1952). Quite systematically, he followed the sequential steps that da Vinci had advised a young artist to follow. These were: to establish a competence for drawing; to learn perspective; to understand the proportions of objects; to copy from a master (which van Gogh had been doing for some years); to study drawing and painting nature; to observe and analyze the works of masters; and, finally, to practice and re-work a concept again and again.

It appears that van Gogh not only took da Vinci's advice to heart but diligently and continuously applied the latter's precepts to his work. Da Vinci's advice provided a stable framework within which van Gogh could develop multiple competencies, and experiment judiciously. "Drawing is the backbone of painting" was a credo often voiced by him. As already mentioned, he devoted the first two years of the ten-year period entirely to drawing in order to be competent in that skill before taking on the arduous task of mastering oil painting. His goal was to be good enough at drawing so that it would be as easy as writing. He had already read books presenting traditional applications of perspective theory, including Albrecht Dürer's discourse on that subject, first published in 1525. It was from Dürer that van Gogh got the idea of using a perspective frame—a device that allowed the artist to compare the proportions of a nearby object with those of a more distant one. He had also often copied the works of other artists—for example Bargue and Millet—but he now pursued this activity more purposefully. In fact he pursued all these activities more purposefully because they were undertaken within the framework of a larger goal to which he had fully committed himself—that of becoming an artist. This pattern in the work of creative people has been identified by Gruber (1989) as the "organization of purpose" represented in the person's "network of enterprise."

PARIS

The ten years of van Gogh's life as a committed artist can be divided neatly into two periods: from 1880 until 1885 when he worked and lived mostly in Holland, and from 1886–1890 when he lived and worked in France, where he died. From 1886–1888, he and Theo shared an apartment in Paris and there was no need for any correspondence. In the absence of any letters, we have only indirect knowledge of a somewhat turbulent period (de Leeuw, 1997, p. 325).

Van Gogh arrived in Paris at a time of some dissatisfaction with his own work, centering on his use of color, which he considered too limited, too dark, and too morose. He believed that he had gone as far as he wanted to in the use of dark colors and chiaroscuro and the extension of the principles of the Dutch school, represented by Rembrandt and Hals. Theo had described the experimental work of the Impressionists to Vincent and Vincent was curios to see what these people were doing. As an art dealer, Theo had personal contact with the leading Parisian artists of the day, and was able to introduce them to Vincent. Van Gogh had come to Paris to join the Corman atelier and learn what he could. There he met Émile Bernard (with whom he established an extended collaboration), Toulouse-Lautrec, and the Australian John Peter Russell. He also met Paul Signac, with whom he exchanged ideas regarding technique, and compared and discussed each other's work. Together, they worked out a system in which various techniques were coded and designed to represent different surfaces or objects. Dots, for example, represented objects such as roads, trees or water near the horizon. Undulating lines represented turbulent skies or swirling water in the foreground. Dashes represented mid-distance objects, such as a road midway between the foreground and the horizon.

As de Leeuw (1997) points out, van Gogh must have been amazed, when he came to Paris, to see how out of touch his own method of working was with that of his leading contemporaries. He adopted the color theories of the Impressionists and also changed the subject matter of his work, painting the streets and cafés that surrounded him. His Paris sojourn became "a new term of apprenticeship" (p. 327).

ARLES

The Arles period (December 1887–December 1888) was punctuated by the two-month period, November and December 1888, when he and Paul Gauguin lived and worked together.

In February of 1888, van Gogh left Paris for Arles, a relatively small town in Provence in southern France. He longed for sun and warmth, for sun-lit countryside, and felt his health deteriorating in Paris. In a letter to his sister Wil, he said the winter in Pars was too severe and, later, that he was worn out by Paris. Another reason to go to Arles was its pristine natural environment, in contrast to Paris. The Paris scene had become somewhat stale. Arles represented a new field of artistic action.

Van Gogh kept in touch with Émile Bernard through Theo. Bernard was close to Paul Gauguin, who was also in bad health and short of money. Van Gogh then had the idea of establishing a colony where artists would live and work together and exchange ideas and techniques. The colony would be different from existing schools in that the artists would teach each other and be free of the influence of academic strictures and art dealers. It would create a new method of working and a new life style for the artist. Van Gogh strongly believed in learning from but also breaking with tradition. He suggested that Theo and Tersteeg become the "experts" in this enterprise, lending it credence and investing capital in it and, in return, would each year be given a certain number of paintings with a certain value by the artist members of the cooperative. Paul Gauguin would become the head of the colony and Theo would be a kind of administrative coordinator. Van Gogh had been impressed artistically and personally by Gauguin when they known each other in Paris. He saw his dream of establishing an artist's colony as beginning with a cooperative working with Gauguin in Arles.

Van Gogh exchanged letters, works of art and ideas with potential collaborators. He also concentrated on developing his skills as an artist. During the day, he worked on drawings and paintings—landscapes, still lifes, and portraits—and in the evening he wrote letters to collaborators. He worked as few have worked—hard and fast. During the 15 months he was in Arles, just 444 days, he produced over 200 paintings and over 100 drawings, demonstrating that, for him, being creative meant intense, protracted activity. Mastery was arduous and continuous. Van Gogh was critical of his own work and did not often consider his paintings good by his own standards. However, he came to believe that the paintings finished quickly, in one long session, were his best. He declared that while he might have completed them very fast, he had given them a lot of thought before putting brush to paper (de Leeuw, 1997, p. 373).

Van Gogh had met Gauguin in Paris and the two had remained in contact. Theo was Gauguin's art dealer and in February, 1888, Vincent wrote to Theo "I have had a letter from Gauguin telling me that he has been in bed for a fortnight; that he is on the rocks, as he has had to pay some crying debts and wants to know if you have sold anything for him; he is so pressed for a little money that he would be ready to reduce the price of his pictures still further (Stone, 1937, p. 331.) Van Gogh empathized and sympathized with Gauguin's reports of his ill health; he too had been ill. He saw Gauguin as both a friend and a symbol for the artist's life of sacrifice and ill-health. He believed that he had a responsibility to help his friend regain his health; all the more reason, in Van Gogh's mind, to have Gauguin come to Arles. He went on, in the same letter:

> Poor Gauguin has no luck. I am very much afraid that in his case convalescence will be even longer, and I am heartily sorry for his plight, especially now that his health is shaken. He hasn't the kind of temperament that profits by hardships; on the contrary, this will only knock him up, and that will spoil him for his work. My God! Shall we see a generation of artists with healthy bodies? (Stone, 1937, p. 332.)

Van Gogh continued to think about having Gauguin come and live with him. He convinced Theo to send money to help Gauguin in Paris. The ever-supportive Theo was thus not only sending money to Vincent but now also to Gauguin. In the summer of 1888, van Gogh wrote to his brother:

> I have had a letter from Gauguin who says he has got from you a letter enclosing fifty francs, which touched him greatly. He seems to be very depressed...he readily agrees to the advantages there would be in living together...I think a society of impressionists could be created, and while it lasted we could live courageously and produce, and that the gains as well as the losses should be taken in common. I am hoping to maintain my argument of last winter, when we talked of an association of artists...The great revolution: art for the artists! (Stone, 1937, pp. 350–351.)

Van Gogh dreamed of an artists' colony where ideas and art could flourish. Although he fervently hoped Gauguin would come, he also did not want to pressure him to move if Gauguin really hoped to do something better in Paris. Van Gogh wanted companionship for artistic, spiritual, and practical reasons. The cost of keeping a household could be defrayed by sharing those costs with another person.[2] He had always thought it "idiotic" for a painter to live alone and, in practical terms, the money he spent could stretch to profit someone else. There would be satisfaction in sharing the daily chores and keeping two or three people going instead of one. All this would serve as the beginning of an association in which the collective would manage and sell their own work rather than putting it all into the hands of unscrupulous dealers. The plan to establish a painters'

---

[2] Van Gogh also liked women and would have liked to live with a woman he loved. Based on previous failed relationships, however, he believed that he was unsuited to meet the needs of a woman, not to mention the fact that such an arrangement would have interfered with his ideas of an artists' colony.

cooperative of impressionists was ever on van Gogh's mind. It crops up in letters to Theo, to his fellow artists and to his sister Wil, whether he is mentioning that he had just read a book on the German composer Richard Wagner and was interested that Wagner's ideas about "community" were so consonant with his own, or complaining of the low social and economic status of painters. To Wil he wrote:

> We live in an unspeakably awful and miserable world for artists. The exhibitions, the shops selling pictures, everything, everything is in the hands of people who grab all the money. (de Leeuw, 1997, p. 367.)

At the same time, these letters are also full of his work—descriptions of his paintings, the colors he is using for the various objects, his evaluation of them, his ideas about them and broader artistic issues. He describes painting in the midday heat, how to protect one's easel from being blown over by the famous *mistral* (as the seasonal wind is called), how different he looked now compared to the man he depicted in a self-portrait he had painted in Paris. Everywhere, in these letters, his passion for art is on display

At the end of June 1888, Theo wrote to Vincent that Gauguin had finally agreed to come to Arles and share a house with Vincent. It was not until several months later—in October—that Gauguin actually arrived. On October 3rd, 1888 van Gogh wrote to Gauguin and told him how as he worked he had still been thinking of the two of them "setting up a studio" together (de Leeuw, 1997, p. 412). He also said that he was working feverishly. Indeed, he was worn out and forced to rest for a few days. Eventually, the intense pace of his activities in summer and autumn exhausted him so much that "he felt he was 'reduced once more close to the deranged state of Hugo van der Goes in the painting by Émile Wauters'" (de Leeuw, 1997, p. 416). Considering what was to come, this remark was prescient.

Gauguin eventually arrived on October 23. He stayed exactly nine weeks. In a letter to Theo, Vincent seemed weighed down by his debt to his brother and by the fact that his paintings were not selling. He noted that Gauguin's arrival had turned his mind away from the feeling that he was going to be ill.

At first the two painters worked well together. They painted the same local people, spent evenings out together in a cafe, went to a local brothel together and, under Gauguin's influence, van Gogh even painted some works from memory. But there were fundamental differences between the two, and they argued endlessly and disagreed about basic issues in art and the functioning and purposes of the artist. Each had very strong opinions about how the artist should work. Gauguin believed that a work should be conceived as a whole before it was begun and he advised others to have the painting fully worked out before touching the canvas, emphasizing memory and its imaginative translation to the canvas. Van Gogh, the realist, liked to work "from nature"—the scene in front of him. He also believed that colors should have psychological significance, and not merely play a decorative role in a painting. Gauguin believed in working slowly and deliberately; van Gogh believed in going to the main theme of the painting and working with an exalted rapidity.[3] Gauguin painted a portrait of Vincent to which the latter had a violently negative response "It's certainly me but me gone mad" (de Leeuw, 1997, p. 423). A week later, after a loud argument in a café, van Gogh allegedly threw a glass of absinthe at Gauguin, an incident that was apparently smoothed over but not forgotten. In a letter written to Theo in the latter half of December, which included a vivid description of a gallery he and Gauguin had visited in Montpelier, van Gogh wrote:

> Gauguin and I discuss Delacroix, Rembrandt, etc., a great deal. The debate is *exceedingly electric* and sometimes when we finish our minds are as drained as an electric battery after discharge. (NYGS, 1978, Letter 564.)

On December 23, van Gogh writes again to Theo, this time a much briefer letter:

> I think that Gauguin was a little disenchanted with the good town of Arles...and above all with me...Indeed, there are serious problems to overcome here still, for him as well as for me...But these problems lie more in ourselves than anywhere else. In short I think that he'll either simply leave or he'll simply stay. I've told him to think it over and weigh up the pros and cons before doing anything. Gauguin is very strong, very creative...I await his decision with absolute equanimity (NYGS, 1978, Letter 565, 23 December, 1888).

This very calm and rational letter was followed the same evening by an emotionally quite different event. Gauguin was taking a walk when van Gogh suddenly appeared and threatened him with a razor. Gauguin calmed him down, but decided to stay the night in a local hotel. Later that night, van Gogh appeared at the brothel he frequented and asked for a prostitute called Rachel. He gave her a piece of his earlobe which he had sliced from his ear and asked her to look after it. Police found him the next morning unconscious in his bed. This account comes mainly from Gauguin and also, "bit by bit" from van Gogh. (de Leeuw, 1997, pp. 425–426).

---

[3] Indeed, while he was in Arles, van Gogh painted as many as three paintings a day, some in as little as 45 minutes, according to his accounts; in Paris his swift execution had amazed his teachers and fellow students.

Vincent apparently had had some kind of a seizure or psychotic episode. Allegedly, he seemed dazed and bewildered, and perhaps drunk, when he appeared at the brothel. The injury to his ear had severed an artery. He returned home and the police, summoned by people at the brothel, found him in bed the next morning. He had lost an enormous amount of blood.

Van Gogh recovered gradually. His depression about what had happened and his fear of another attack weighed on him. But he soon discovered that he had not lost his passion for painting and began to paint again in March of 1889. He conjectured that his "attack" may have been brought on by alcohol and even tobacco, but he continued to drink and smoke. He seemed unable to organize his life and reluctant to set up a studio by himself. He had lost a lot of his work as a result of floods and damp while he was in the hospital. He also believed that the loss of his studio, Gauguin's departure, and the end of his ideas of collaborative work with others were his fault. Theo was worried about his brother's feelings of guilt and inadequacy and the possibility of suicide. He constantly tried to reassure him and pointed out that he, Theo, had had a very good year and money was not a problem. Vincent considered admitting himself to an asylum, in the hope that further attacks might be prevented.

SAINT-RÉMY AND AUVERS-SUR-OISE

Van Gogh closed out the final 14 months of his life in St. Rémy, where he lived in a mental institution, being treated for seizures, and in Auvers-sur-Oise, where he was in the care of Dr. Paul Gachet. At the mental hospital in Saint Rémy, he continued to paint, except when he was having an attack. He never worked during such episodes and never put brush to canvas until he was completely recovered. Since there were plenty of empty rooms in the asylum, he was given an additional room in which to work. In May, 1889, he wrote Theo that "my *fear* of madness is wearing off markedly." In the same letter, he takes comfort from what he learns and sees in the asylum:

> I am so grateful for yet another thing. I've noticed that others, too, hear sounds and strange voices during their attacks, as I did, and that things seemed to change before their very eyes. And that lessened the horror with which I remembered my first attack, something that, when it comes upon you unexpectedly, cannot but frighten you terribly. Once you know it is part of the illness, you accept it like anything else (NYGS, 1978, Letter 592, 22 May, 1889).

These are the comments of a keen objective intelligence; and they reflect van Gogh the painter as well: combining dispassionate observation and analysis with the emotional expression of subjective experience.

Van Gogh produced many masterpieces at this time. Sadly, he had another attack in July and could not return to work until August. By September he was more cheerful and wrote to Theo:

> My work is going very well, I am finding things that I have sought in vain for years, and feeling this, I am always thinking of that saying of Delacroix's that you know, namely that he discovered painting when he no longer had any breath or teeth left. (NYGS, 1978, Letter 605, 10 September 1889.)

At this point, his skills were such that he could rapidly produce a rendition of a work in the style of Delacroix. He wrote "if you could see me working, my brain so clear and my fingers so sure that I have drawn that 'Pieta' by Delacroix without taking a single measurement" (Letter 605, 10 September 1889).

Theo sent his brother reproductions of paintings by Rembrandt, Millet and Delacroix, which Vincent used as the basis for his own work, no longer copying but "painting" them. During this period he produced some of his finest painting. The image of the miner was still perhaps a central one for van Gogh; but it now took on a different guise in view of his own illness so that he saw himself "like a miner who is always in danger [and] makes haste in what he does." (NYGS, 1978, Letter 610, 1889).

In December of 1889, van Gogh had another attack followed by still another in January of 1990 and a third a few weeks later. During his last week in Saint Rémy, he finished four still lifes with flowers. He had already told Theo that he wanted to move to Auvers. In Saint Rémy, where he had lived for a year, he was overwhelmed by "boredom and grief" (de Leeuw, 1997, p. 485). He went to Auvers-sur-Oise via Paris because he wanted to meet his new sister-in-law who had recently married Theo, as well as their son, named after Vincent. Johanna van Gogh was surprised to see not a sick man but a "sturdy broad-shouldered man, with a healthy colour, a smile on his face and a very resolute appearance" (de Leeuw, 1997, p. 488). Van Gogh was very happy to see Theo and Theo's family but he worried about his brother's chronic cough. He left Paris after three days and went to Auvers where he was put in the care of Dr. Gachet, a psychiatrist, homeopathic physician and amateur artist.

Van Gogh's output during what would be the last two months of his life was remarkable. In July, he wrote to Theo:

> I have set to work again—although the brush is nearly falling from my hands—and because I knew exactly what I wanted to do, I have

painted three more large canvases. They are vast stretches of wheat under troubled skies, and I didn't have to put myself out very much in order to try and express sadness and extreme loneliness. (NYGS, 1978, Letter 649 c.10 July, 1890.)

Van Gogh shot and wounded himself among those wheat fields on July 27, 1890. Theo was summoned and his brother seemed to be improving when he fell into a coma and died in Theo's presence on July 29.[4]

VAN GOGH'S SOCIAL INTERACTIONS AND COMPARISONS

At the beginning of this chapter I introduced social comparison theory and three of its constructs—upward comparison, downward comparison, and lateral comparison. I now want to consider how these comparison categories can be applied to van Gogh's development as an artist and a person.

Upward Social Comparison

One does not have to know the people one compares oneself with; indeed, they can be distant strangers or long dead. Nevertheless, it is clear that van Gogh's years as a fully committed artist were richly populated with other artists and members of the art world. In a letter to Theo, van Gogh asked how anyone can learn if no-one shows the way. With all the

best intentions in the world, one cannot succeed without coming into contact with artists who are more advanced. (NYGS, 1978, Letter 138, November, 1980.)

This letter expresses the need for knowledge of a neophyte. Actually, van Gogh was not exactly such a neophyte since, as in many respects an autodidact, he had been sketching for many years on his own. He admired many artists, some of whom became important influences at different points in his own development. The first of these, in his formative

---

[4] It is important to remember that the Impressionists, Post-Impressionists, and Neo-Impressionists are considered as groups, as if the work in each group was somehow the same. In fact, members in each group had in common only that they lived and worked at about the same and applied a novel set of principles to their work. But each member of each group had a unique voice and style and when we see or think of the work of van Gogh, Gauguin, Toulouse-Lautrec, and Bonnard—all post-impressionists—it is their differences that strike us rather than their similarities.

phase as an artist, was Anton Mauve, himself an eminent artist. Mauve had married into the Van Gogh family so he was not only known to van Gogh as someone who knew much more about art than he, but as someone who might also be more readily available as a teacher because of the family connection. So from Mauve he learned basic skills and technique, especially in drawing and water-coloring. He wrote to Theo about:

> a drawing... made at Mauve's studio, and really the best watercolor I had, especially because Mauve had put some touches in it, and had watched me make it and drawn my attention to some points. (Stone, p. 135)

There were many other artists whom van Gogh looked up to: Leonardo da Vinci, from whom he learned how to sequence his early learning–drawing, perspective, understanding the proportions of an object, copying from a master, and so on; what he learned from da Vinci, became part of van Gogh's organization of knowledge (Gruber, 1989). He learned from Rembrandt (especially chiaroscuro); and from Gauguin whose impasto technique (the thick application of paint), he admired and used. In Daumier, he found confirmation of his love of depicting the common person. From Millet he found inspiration, and copied and later painted copies of Millet's work. From the Japanese artist Hokusai, he learned to use line in dynamic ways. Van Gogh's admiration of Rembrandt and Millet went beyond composition and technique; the emotions expressed by these painters' works also provided a model for what van Gogh wanted to express emotionally in his own works. He knew the work of all these artists and knew he needed their knowledge by gauging what they had that he wanted to emulate in his own work in his own way.

Sometimes, the variety and many-layered impact of such figures surely included a process of "trying-on" the actual work of the admired artist by copying, or drawing or painting *in the manner of* that person. This is both an attempt at mastery as well as a testing out of what it feels like to "be" that artist. It may provide a special experience in artistic development that enables the person to learn from and assimilate these new knowledge experiences selectively.

Apart from copying them, van Gogh routinely looked at and analyzed the works of great artists. In Paris he often visited the Louvre and constantly went to exhibitions showing the work of contemporary artists. While Gauguin was in Arles, van Gogh and he regularly visited nearby museums to see and discuss the art of others. This, of course, is a common activity among nearly all creative people—the need to re-view existing products in their field to learn or re-learn; and the need to compare their own work with that of their contemporaries.

Downward Social Comparison

In this category, a person compares his or her skills, values, performance, etc., with those of someone else and comes out ahead. The mo-
tive here, through negation, is often self-enhancement rather than self-
evaluation. When there is a threat to one's psychological well-being, it can
be helpful to compare oneself to someone who is worse off in order to
feel better about one's own situation. Rejecting the values of someone else
can also go hand-in-hand with a reaffirmation of one's own values and
self-image.

Van Gogh rejected his art dealer Tersteeg's suggestion that he paint
"things that sell." To follow Tersteeg's suggestion would be a moral be-
trayal of his artistic goals and practices. Van Gogh rejected art that, in
his eyes, had no merit but appealed to public taste. Having worked for
Tersteeg himself, and having both an uncle and a brother who were art
dealers, he learned what sold and what didn't. He had worked hard to
learn the principles of perspective, proportion, and on his drawing. It was
as though Tersteeg's comment trivialized all that he was doing. Tersteeg
helped to clarify van Gogh's ideas about what he did and did not want to
do. Even when he badly needed money, van Gogh refused to compromise
this principle. To Theo, he said "I would as soon be, say, a hotel waiter as
the kind of watercolour manufacturer some of the Italians are" (Richter,
1997, p. 182)

The arguments with Gauguin also helped van Gogh concretize his
ideas about how he did and did not want to paint. The work of a particular school can also serve as the target of downward comparison. When
Gauguin arrived in Paris in 1886, he was confronted, for the first time, with
the work of his contemporaries. The Impressionists, no longer in the *avant
garde*, had their last group show in that year, and the Post-Impressionists
and Neo-Impressionists were now the *avant garde*. Van Gogh, meeting his
contemporaries and seeing so much of their art, put aside what he had been
doing, and changed what he painted and the colors he used. He put Millet
and painters of rural life behind him (at least for the time being) and became
an apprentice again. He adopted the color theories of the Impressionists
and painted Paris—urban scenes, cafés and streets. Thus his negative evaluation of his previous focus compared with that of his contemporaries led
to a quite different orientation to his work.

Lateral Social Comparison

This category of social comparison is directed at peers, collaborators,
or those who are, in some important respect, equal. The first person who

comes to mind here is Theo van Gogh and what we can deduce from Vincent's letters to him. Vincent poured all his thoughts about his work into these letters. He was intensely focused on his work and thought about it constantly. He sent Theo many sketches and described his paintings in detail, what he thought of them, what the ideas behind them were, what colors he intended to use or had used, and so on. Theo, who was himself an artist as well as an art dealer, must have contributed with comments in reply to Vincent's thoughts about his work. Theo's encouragement of his brother was certainly practical, that is, he gave him money and supplies for his work; but Theo also reliably gave Vincent psychological support. And Vincent, characteristically, offered his ideas and work to Theo in order to learn from him. No doubt, the correspondence with his brother was an important part of van Gogh's own artistic and personal development, in which the comparison of ideas played an important part.

Another important peer comparison and collaboration process was van Gogh's work in Paris with Paul Signac who became an important member of the Neo-Impressionists. These two artists developed a "textural coding" system together—dashes, dots, curves etc., to depict objects in their drawings and paintings. This experience and the work it produced entailed an apparently equal and mutually satisfactory exchange of ideas and suggestions which was certainly reflected in van Gogh's subsequent work.

Van Gogh's work with Gauguin, in addition to its downward comparison also included lateral comparison because each painted the same subjects, for example, the owner of the café which they frequented, and the café itself. Seeing and discussing their two versions of these subjects would, in the most concrete way, clarify similarities and differences in style and technique as well as their different goals for their paintings and what they wanted to render on the canvas. A new idea might emerge from the pooling of their individual perceptions and renditions.

Lateral comparison played a striking role in van Gogh's private life. After he entered the asylum in Saint Rémy, he found people like him there, who had symptoms and terrors similar to his. He found this comforting, counted himself "very grateful" to have learned this and was able to put aside his terrible memories of his first attack and its symptoms because he now knew they were just "part of the illness." As a result, he was able to stop thinking about his condition all the time. Thus, by gaining a less threatening perspective, van Gogh was able to focus more successfully on his work. Comparison with Delacroix, an important artist for van Gogh, served a somewhat similar function. With his work going "very well" some months later, he wrote Theo that he kept thinking of Delacroix's remark that he had discovered painting when he had neither breath nor teeth left. One can produce great work even when one is weak, old, or ill.

CONCLUSION

The three forms of social comparison that I have discussed in this paper all contributed to the development of Vincent van Gogh's work and to his evolving self image as artist and person. With his teachers and mentors (living and dead), he learned basic skills and techniques. By comparing himself with them, he could gauge his progress—seeing what he had learned and what he still wanted to learn from them. His downward comparisons made clear for him what he rejected as part of the artistic enterprise—whether ideas of how to sell one's work (Tersteeg), or ideas and principles of how an artist should construct a work (Gauguin). The rejection can be permanent, or for the time being (as it was for van Gogh's turning away from Millet in Paris). Perhaps, establishing what one is *not* is the beginning of finding out what one is. Lateral comparisons function to differentiate oneself, clarifying differences as well as similarities, as van Gogh did with Gauguin and other Post-Impressionists. Lateral comparison can also function as a comfort oneself when feeling threatened (the asylum, Delacroix).

The work of a highly creative person, in whatever field, is, in part, a history of that person's effort to find a unique voice and construct a new point of view. In the comparison processes, we can see van Gogh doing just that.

From this account, it seems clear that Charles Kuralt's description of van Gogh as a "loner" was off the mark. Of course, when drawing or painting, van Gogh was often alone. Creative work demands solitude; but it is not wholly solitary. As we have seen in the case of van Gogh, his mental and actual world was populated with people who were indispensable to the development of his work. With Theo as anchor, and often as conduit, they represented a shifting reference group, consisting of artists and members of the art establishment. At different times throughout his career he copied and studied their work, discussed art with them, corresponded with them, worked with them, and thought about them. As a social presence in his mind, these people helped him to form his artistic identity and his purposeful development as an artist

CHRONOLOGICAL OUTLINE

1853   Vincent Willem van Gogh born at Groot-Zundert, Holland on March 30, oldest son of the Reverend Theodorus van Gogh and Anna Cornelia Carbentus

1857   Birth of his favorite brother Theodorus (Theo) on May 1

1853–68	Childhood and meager education, one year at village school, two years at boarding school, one and a half years in high school
1869	Joins international art dealers, Goupil & Co in The Hague as their youngest employee
1872	Begins regular correspondence from The Hague with Theo
1873–76	Works at various branches of Goupil & Co in Brussels, London, and Paris. Is dismissed from Goupil's in 1876
1877	Works in a bookshop in Dordrecht, then moves to Amsterdam to prepare for theological examination
1878	Abandons theological studies and moves to the Borinage to work as a lay preacher among the miners. Is later dismissed
1879	In July, decides to become an artist
1880–82	Early development as an artist. Studies with Anton Mauve in The Hague
1883–86	Moves to his parents in Nuenen. Paints weavers, begins work on still lifes, paints portraits of peasants
1886–88	Lives in Paris with Theo, works at Cormon's studio, makes friends with Henri de Toulouse-Lautrec, Émile Bernard and others, meets Gauguin, Pissarro and Seurat. Paints many pictures of Paris life as well as still lifes with flowers
1888	Exhausted by pressures of life in Paris and longing for sun and rest, he moves to Arles, collaborates with Gauguin and, after a violent argument with him, has his first seizure on 23 December, slicing off part of his earlobe. He recovers rapidly
1889	Voluntarily admits himself to a mental hospital in Saint Rémy, works steadily between attacks
1890	Having been declared fit enough, he goes to Auvers-sur-Oise for treatment by Dr. Gachet, a physician and amateur artist. Shoots himself in the chest on July 27. Dies on July 29 in Theo's presence
1891	Theo dies on January 25 at the age of 33

REFERENCES

Buunk, B. & Gibbons, F.X. (Eds.) (1997). *Health, coping and well-being: Perspectives from social comparison theory*. Mahwah, NJ: Lawrence Erlbaum Associates.

De Leeuw, R. (Ed.) (1997). *The letters of Vincent van Gogh*, Trans. A Pomerans. New York: Penguin Putnam.

Festinger, L. (1954). A theory of social comparison processes. *Human Relations*, 114–140.

Gruber, H.E. (1981). *Darwin on man*. Chicago: Chicago University Press.

Gruber, H.E., & Davis, S. (1988). Inching our way up mount Olympus: the evolving systems approach to creative thinking. In Robert Sternberg (Ed.), *The nature of creativity: Contemporary Psychological perspectives*, pp. 298–321. Cambridge, MA: Cambridge University Press.

Gruber, H.E. (1989). The evolving systems approach to creative work. In Doris B. Wallace & Howard E. Gruber (Eds.), *Creative people at work: Twelve cognitive case studies*. New York: Oxford University Press.

New York Graphic Society. (1978). *The complete letters of Vincent van Gogh*, 3 vols. Boston: Little Brown.

Richter, I.A. (Ed.) (1952). *The notebooks of Leonardo da Vinci*. New York: Oxford University Press.

Stone, I. (1937). *Dear Theo* New York: Doubleday.

Suls, J.M. & Wheeler, L. (Eds.) (2000). *Handbook of social comparison theory and research*. New York: Plenum.

Treble, R. (1975). *Van Gogh and his art*. New York: Galahad Books.

Wallace, D. B., & Gruber, H. E. (Eds.) (1989). *Creative people at work: Twelve cognitive case studies*: New York: Oxford University Press.

Wayment, H.A., & Taylor, S.E. (1995). Self-evaluation processes. *Journal of Personality*, 63, pp. 729–757.

Wills, T.A. (1981). Downward comparison principles in social psychology. *Psychological Bulletin*, 90, pp. 245–271.

5

THE EVOLVING SYSTEMS APPROACH AND NARRATIVE THERAPY FOR INCARCERATED MALE YOUTH

Laura Tahir

INTRODUCTION

Substance abuse, AIDS, mental illness, racial oppression, family instability, violence, ennui, crime, and homelessness are some of the ills familiar to inner-city and suburban youth whose neighborhoods have deteriorated and who may end up calling a 6 1/2 × 10-foot prison cell their home. In the last 30 years the number of state prisoners in this country has increased 500 percent (Butterfield, 2002). Even as crime decreased in the 1990s, jail and prison populations grew each year due to stricter sentencing laws. Furthermore, Chaiklin (2001) notes the increasing number of homeless people populating jails and describes one of the functions of jail as an "alternative shelter" for the mentally ill. Unfortunately, incarceration is at times preferred by people, mentally ill or not, who have nowhere better to go.

The purpose of this paper is to apply the evolving systems approach and the narrative techniques of clinical psychology to the study of in-carcerated young men. I will describe a Life Review Group in which a small number of inmates focus on networks of enterprise, construction of a point of view, and identity development. There will be no attempt to give an overview of incarceration nor any sweeping statements about men in prison. Rather, details of particular cases will be presented as they illustrate the evolving systems approach and narrative therapy. The goal is to show how a model that has traditionally been used to study individuals known for remarkable achievement can also be used to understand and treat people who have known little success.

THE EVOLVING SYSTEMS APPROACH

The evolving systems approach (see Gruber, 1980; Gruber & Davis, 1988; Wallace & Gruber, 1989) has been a means to scrutinize the creative work of extraordinary individuals. The emphasis has been on the uniqueness of the creative person, the development of creative work, and the creative product(s). The creative process is demystified through the examination of single cases. The merits of this idiographic approach as well as the contributions of the nomothetic approach to the study of creativity (and personality in general) have been reviewed elsewhere (e.g., Wallace, 1989; Tahir, 1996).

The evolving systems approach to creative work focuses on facets of the development of the creator, his or her work, and the contextual frame in which this work occurs. Three interrelated subsystems interact in the development of the creative work: knowledge, purpose, and affect.

The organization of knowledge refers to the structures of the creative individual's thought. Creative thought does not take place during "one great moment of insight," nor is it "one monotonic gradual change" (Gruber, 1977, p. 6). It is a process, characterized by repetition and perseverance, in which structures evolve. The organization of purpose concerns the way a person orchestrates his or her activities in a network of enterprise that is crucial to the productive work and life. The organization of affect refers to the creative person's feelings—the passion for the work, the many struggles and failures, the joy of functioning optimally. The construction and maintenance of an appropriate affective system makes for steady creative work and nurtures the creative process. Positive emotions such as curiosity, hope, the joy of discovery, and love of truth are all motivators essential to the maintenance of an ongoing creative system.

If the evolving systems approach can describe and analyze extraordinarily creative work, what can it tell us about the failures of that process? A single life story can have episodes of struggle, disappointment, and failure, as well as triumph and transcendence. The chapters of our storied lives may be about wealth or poverty, stability or disarray, anger or contentment, success or bitter defeat. The examples I present in this paper are those of developing young lives in periods of distress due to incarceration. The young men described here were unable to conform to the laws of society. Brower's (1999) work on creative people who were incarcerated at some point in their lives applies the evolving systems approach to understand their failure to conform. The subjects in his study were noted for their positive contributions to society and recognized unequivocally as extraordinary. The young men illustrated here, however, have primarily witnessed defeat and have not experienced noteworthy success.

When a system is malfunctioning—when a young man becomes a drug addict and desperately steals jewelry from his grandmother or, when on a whim, someone carjacks an innocent stranger—one might explain this behavior by looking at the failure of the subsystems of knowledge, purpose, and affect. An attitude devoid of moral reflection indicates a damaged knowledge system. Apathy is symptomatic of a deadened sense of purpose, and a network of enterprise in such a case would be anemic and have no meaningful organization at all. A crime of passion is affect gone awry, a failure of self-control; at the other extreme, the "banality of evil" is possible when the development of empathy is stunted and affect is blunted.

NARRATIVE THERAPY

The evolving systems approach, although using a clinical method has primarily served the academic study of creative work rather than for applications such as teaching or psychotherapy. Of the various schools and methods of clinical psychology, the ones most compatible with the evolving systems approach can be loosely grouped under the label "narrative therapy."

Narrative therapy is usually associated with the work of Michael White and David Epston (e.g., White & Epston, 1990). Their focus on the uniqueness of personality and the possibility of change is phenomenological, idiographic, and pluralistic. Describing the work of White and Epston and their colleagues, O'Hanlon (1994) referred to it as "psychotherapy's third wave." The first wave, which began with Freud, was pathology-focused and powered by what O'Hanlon called "our delusion that we could determine what was sick or healthy, right or wrong" (p. 22). The second wave attempted to counter this perspective with problem-focused therapies such as behavioral therapy, cognitive therapy, and family therapy, which teach that faulty patterns of conduct, thought, and communication can be changed, as opposed to believing that people are "sick" and need to be "cured." Third wave therapies are competence-based. The emphasis is on showing clients how to provide their own solutions. Rather than focusing on individual pathology or interpersonal troubles, narrative therapists, through various creative techniques, help people to externalize their situations, to see how the details of their lives are social and personal constructions, and to be open to their ability to effect change. The evolving systems approach too is competence-based in its emphasis on the creative individual at work rather than as a recipient of a gift of the muse.

The evolving systems approach and narrative psychotherapy approaches rely on what Geertz (1973) referred to as "thick" description which, in contrast to "thin" description, portrays the meaning of an event to the person who experienced it. Thick description reveal what particular events mean to the person. Thin description distorts in ways that are socially and culturally defined. Gruber (1980) referred to the necessity of thick description and advised us to attend closely to the introspections of our subject and our subject's subject when he quotes Albert Einstein, "If atoms could talk, I would surely listen" (p. 276). My task in this chapter is to use thick description to scrutinize a group of distressed young inmates.

THE NARRATIVE METAPHOR AND CONSTRUCTION OF IDENTITY IN ADOLESCENCE

Psychologists studying the concept of identity or self have used such metaphors as stream (James, 1890/1902), or actor on the stage (Goffman, 1959), or acorn becoming an oak (Mazlow, 1968). In recent years the narrative metaphor has gained great popularity. Bruner (1986) argued that the narrative metaphor of self captures the idea of the self not as a static entity that can be objectively perceived but as one that evolves only as it is narrated. He argued that there are two modes of cognitive functioning, the narrative and the paradigmatic, each providing a distinctive way of ordering experience, and each irreducible (although complementary) to the other. He noted that we know far more about the paradigmatic mode than the narrative mode.

The narrative mode of knowing is an experience of particulars rather than constructs about variables and classes. It leads to "good stories, gripping drama, believable (though not necessarily 'true') historical accounts" (Bruner, 1986. p. 13). The paradigmatic or logico-scientific mode transcends the particular and "employs categorization or conceptualization and the operations by which categories are established, instantiated, idealized, and related one to the other to form a system" (p. 12). The aim of paradigmatic thinking is to argue or establish "truth" rather than meaning. The narrative mode seeks "verisimilitude" or "lifelikeness." What enables this process to occur is what Bruner described as subjunctivizing reality.

Three features are triggered by good narrative that enlist the reader's imagination and thereby subjunctivize reality. The first is the creation of implicit rather than explicit meanings. Implicit meaning goes beyond the text, requiring the reader to interact with the text. "It is the 'relative indeterminacy of text' that allows a spectrum of actualizations," and "with explicitness, the reader's degrees of interpretive freedom are annulled" (Bruner, 1986. p. 25). The second feature is subjectification, "the depiction of reality not through an omniscient eye that views a timeless reality, but through the filter of the consciousness of protagonists in the story" (p. 25). Bruner noted that in Joyce's *Dubliners* we see "reality" only through the eyes of the characters. The third feature of good narrative is what Bruner called multiple perspective, "beholding the world not univocally but simultaneously through a set of prisms each of which catches some part of it" (Bruner, 1986 p. 26).

The concept of subjunctivizing reality is what has attracted psychotherapists to the narrative metaphor and narrative therapy (e.g., White & Epston, 1990; Parry & Doan, 1994). The narrative mode creates good stories that enable us to form "conclusions not about certainties in an aboriginal world, but about the varying perspectives that can be constructed to make experience comprehensible" (Bruner 1986, p. 37). Psychotherapists note that the paradigmatic mode offers a weak means to describe the complexity of human behavior. It is to psychotherapy's detriment that "in its efforts to legitimize itself as truly scientific and hence 'truthful,' [it] still tends to theorize scientifically for an activity that is inescapably narrative in its subject matter, thereby establishing the foundations of its practice exclusively in paradigmatic language" (Parry & Doan, 1994 p. 4).

"To be in the subjunctive mode" according to Bruner, "is to be trafficking in human possibilities rather than in settled certainties" (Bruner, 1986, p. 26). The actual text needs subjunctivity so that the reader can create a world of her own. This is what Bruner is referring to when he agrees with Barthes that the writer's greatest gift to the reader is to help him or her become a writer. This is a liberating concept that invites psychotherapists to imagine a better world: the therapist's greatest gift to the client is to help him or her become a therapist.

In the narrative mode, meaning is constructed through social discourse. Harré (1984) conceptualized "personal being" as socially constituted and went so far as to define fundamental human reality as a conversation. This postmodern perspective that the "self" is socially constructed views stories as both effecting and reflecting the construction. This perspective is particularly amenable to group therapy. Knowledge arises in a community of knowers, and is not imparted by an "expert' (e.g., doctor or healer) to the person (e.g., the patient) who is waiting to gain that knowledge by just listening to the "truth." In a prison, narrative group therapy experience means that each inmate constructs a social self—as opposed to having an expert convey knowledge to them about themselves.

Perhaps a caveat is needed here. It is a common prison cliché that "I didn't really do it" refers to every inmate's side of the story. Can one mind all sides of the story and come out knowing the "truth"? Rorty (1991) addressed this question by noting that the "repudiation of the traditional ... image of the human being as Knower does not seem to us to entail that we face an abyss, but merely that we face a range of choices" (p. 132). Postmodernism challenges the objective validity of truth. But if the question is: Can the postmodern thinker accuse the inmate of anything? the answer is that there is certainly a difference between purposeful lies and cultural relativism. In some cases an inmate's narrative may be contaminated by resolute dishonesty. A person who breaks the law and lies about it knows on some level not to trust his own stories because he knows they have been used to distort, cheat, and hurt. He needs to learn to find his voice as an instrument of verisimilitude. He needs to know that stories can describe a phenomenological truth, that they can provide a new possibility.

LIFE REVIEW GROUP

Morgan, Winterowd, and Ferrel (1999) recently reviewed the positive impact of group psychotherapy in prison settings. Their survey examined the benefits of group methods in comparison to individual methods, referring to the therapeutic factors such as group cohesiveness and socialization that are more difficult to create in individual therapy.

The Life Review Group described here took place in a state prison housing approximately 1700 young men (ages 16 to 20s) at all levels of security.[1] The Life Review Group met for 26 weekly 90-minute sessions. The inmates who choose to participate are self-selected, and there are from 6 to 8 in each group. Most group members have been designated as "special needs inmates," meaning they have been given either an Axis I or Axis II diagnosis. During the first session the group members are told that there are only two "rules." The first is that thoughts and feelings will be expressed

---

[1] In order to protect the identity of the inmates involved, their names and details of their lives have been disguised.

in words, not by acting out.[2] Second, the inmates agree that what is said in the group will remain confidential.

Spending much of their formative years incarcerated, the young men in the Life Review Group face the challenge of identity development in an artificial environment. This "home" is usually not thought of as conducive to growth, but at least it provides the basic needs of food and shelter. Through group work focusing on identity construction, it is possible to begin to provide as well for the psychological needs of these men, many of whom have never had the emotional, intellectual, and social opportunities that promote healthy development. In addition to the stressors of incarceration and their presenting symptoms of mental disorder, such as anxiety, panic, obsessions, and depression, incarcerated special needs adolescents and young adults may be experiencing natural developmental crises. They may present with anger rather than depression, or arrogance rather than desperation. They experience little, if any, awareness that part of their struggle is due to identity confusion, missed opportunities to explore who they are and what they are doing in life. The men in the Life Review Group have said that "crime is everywhere," and that their neighborhoods are "drug-infested." They identify themselves with impoverishment and appear trapped in narratives of hopeless struggle and unmet needs. Crime often seems to be all they know.

During the first session of the Life Review Group the leader explains the purpose of the group, which is to get people to construct a meaningful life story. The group is presented with the idea of network of enterprise and are asked to describe the various enterprises of their own lives. They are also introduced to the ideas of organization of affect and organization of knowledge. Questions are provided about specific events in early childhood, and the inmates are asked to recall their earliest memories. They are encouraged to make connections between these early experiences and their later networks of enterprise. Depending on each individual's own level of comfort with the group, disturbing or happy or seemingly unremarkable events are described.

The inmates in the Life Review Group found the concepts of organization of purpose and network of enterprise more amenable to discussion than organization of affect or organization of knowledge. While they often found it difficult to articulate feelings or to feel at ease when talking about intellect, they welcomed the opportunity to describe their daily activities.

---

[2] Fine (1973) made the important distinction between poor impulse control and acting out. Whereas most inmates believe they have poor impulse control and know that this gets them into trouble, acting-out behavior—such as sneering at or deliberately shoving someone—is usually experienced by the inmate as under his control.

Describing their actions as enterprises helped them to understand better what they were doing, and finding organization in an enterprise enabled them to see that they were capable of order. They were also confronted with the frailty of their behaviors and came to see much of their activity as mindless venture rather than as enterprise.

Over a 26-week course, the group leader gives exercises to stimulate life review thinking. The goal is thick description. Finding a voice and exploiting the narrative mode is especially difficult for the disenfranchised. When they talk among peers, there is pressure to be "cool," to show that they are distinct from the authorities. But to be "successful" with the people who exercise authority over them, they often feel that they must blindly accept what they are told to think. Then they end up feeling bound by rules rather than governed by them. Their narratives at first are usually characterized by thin description based on what they may have heard from authority figures. In fact, this is part of the socialization of incarceration.

Underprivileged people who want to gain privilege may rebel, or they may resign themselves to hopelessness. Implied in success stories, however, is that learning rules will eventually lead to success. An inmate who is struggling to learn the rules may get stuck in the thin description of established ways of thinking that have been elevated to "wisdom" and can obscure rather than enlighten. DSM diagnoses, for instance, are often accepted as hard facts based on some measure of objectivity rather than as guides to help describe particular behaviors in particular cultures. For example, developmental crises that are peculiar to each individual and may be difficult to understand can be misinterpreted as symptoms of borderline personality disorder, and the real issues get lost in the simplification of that label. An inmate may then compliantly accept a diagnosis without understanding that his troubles are developmental, limiting himself by a definition of pathology that he has been told explains who he is, and closing himself off to the possibility of change.

Another example of implicit wisdom is that of popular notions of what causes behavior. For instance, Inmate JR described to the group how both his grandfather and his father had been drug addicts who had served time in prison. Both had neglected their own sons, and JR was in the process of neglecting his son. With the family system as a guiding metaphor in this case, we might focus on the thin description that a repeated arrangement in this family explains how JR fell into the trap of addiction and abandoning his own child. While this family story can be helpful in understanding patterns, it can also obscure possibilities for change. When self-stories are thin, they need to be re-examined, or "thickened." Given their status of disenfranchisement, most inmates are prime candidates for thin description. They are used to being told what to do, and if they read anything by an "authority," it is given great credence. Inmate JR's thought that he would most likely repeat his father's and grandfather's patterns of child neglect is implied in most of our conceptions of psychology and accepted as "truth" by those whose do not feel they have the right to examine it. The narrative metaphor would lead us to a thick description, the particulars in which JR can recognize that other forces were at play in the trajectory of his 21-year-life. Thick description seeks to avoid the unrecognized power of implicit social norms and assumptions. In fact, JR realized that his story was very different from that of his father and grandfather. By re-examining his stories in the group, he was able to re-define his identity and gain an enlarged sense of possibility.

In addition to projective-type assignments, the inmates in one group also discussed a biographical account of Darryl Strawberry in which they came to understand the concept of underachievement in a nationally known fallen hero. Such an account can offer indirect contribution to a person's developing sense of self. Adolescents are quick to identify with popular characters, and by closely examining the lives of such people, both flaws and positive attributes become available to be assimilated as chosen.

One important function of group work is to relieve stress through disclosure of feelings related to past trauma. Inmates in youth facilities as a rule come from troubled backgrounds and have had little chance to learn to articulate their experience or express their feelings about their experience. Often they have been victims of sexual or physical trauma. Richards, Beal, Seagal, and Pennabaker (2000) assessed the health effects of disclosure of traumatic events in a group of maximum-security male prison inmates in the Midwest and showed that men in a trauma writing group significantly decreased their infirmary visits for various physical complaints. This aspect of group is part of the Life Review Group. As the inmates' stories evolve, as they get to know each other, they often want to go beyond the trauma and redefine themselves as young adults looking forward to a better life. By talking about the past, remembering their stories, these inmates teach themselves not only the healing power of the narrative, but they learn to know who they are, who they are becoming.

As the Life Review Group progressed, most of the inmates showed increasing willingness to share their experiences. However, not all the inmates were able to tolerate their feelings. One member left after the third group session and explained later in an individual session that he felt he "wasn't ready for the group." He had been able to reveal feelings of neglect by his immature parents, but after admitting that his father once threw him off the windowsill onto the floor, almost pushing him out the window in the process, he had great difficulty maintaining his stance of protection of the family. In such a case the group leader needs to respect the inmate's vulnerability and will ideally arrange to work on these issues individually.

One of the assignments toward the end of the group sessions was for participants to describe their experience of the group. As the result of unexpected parole dates and transfers (uncertainty is the only certainty in a prison), this particular Life Review Group had shrunk from six to two inmates—BK and JR. BK described the growing relationship between him and JR and pointed to the importance of social bonds in forming identity in young adulthood:

> When I first started this group six months ago, I never thought that this group would take me on some of the experiences I have had.
>
> We started out with 6 guys in our group, and a female psych. It's now down to two guys holding on for the change we know we can achieve by thinking more positive and getting in tune with our true selves. I've learned that I wasn't the only one who ran from their problems by using drugs or partying all weekend long. I have also gained more awareness about my depression and how I can have a self talk with myself before giving up on life.
>
> We have covered much written and handout assignments, which helped me to get a better understanding on how we need our childhood and some guidance as we grew up. I realized that my childhood wasn't all that bad that I made it out to be. My teenage yrs I will admit were robbed from me due to partying with older people, using all sorts of drugs and just not giving a damn about living.
>
> One of the first handouts (It's Never Too Late for a Happy Childhood) that were given to us has helped me have confidence in building a new childhood and new emotions within myself. And I must also understand that my childhood even though it was a hard and painful route, it had made me to be the man I came to be today. I can now take my life serious and enjoy being alive and having mental freedom.
>
> I have also been given the opportunity to grow with a good friend, JR. We both can relate to each other's thinking patterns. I feel the growth was meant for the both of us to share and build mentally a sound mind and striving attitude toward living. Who knows exactly where we'll be, but I hope we never lose contact, we owe it to each other to check up on each other's progress in the future. Six months of sharing cannot go to waste.

BK's description demonstrates that the stories a person continually tells him- or herself and others represent the evolving self image he or she has which, in turn, have a powerful influence on the ways in which he or she lives life. The group can provide feedback on each other's stories, pointing out distortions where they seem to exist. Thereby the others, such as JR, become woven into the self-stories.

At the end of the 26-week period, each inmate in the Life Review Group writes his own narrative, the story of his life. The assignments may have been useful in their narratives, but the inmates are not instructed to present their narratives based on any of these assignments. They are also asked to include in this narrative a look at the future and the contributions they may make. Finally, they consider their mortality and write their own obituaries.

Inmate BK

BK is a 22-year-old single male of African-American and Irish descent. He never knew his biological father and was reared, along with his 13 siblings, primarily by his mother. At times he lived with his maternal grandmother or an aunt. His mother had boyfriends from time to time, none of whom were in BK's life long enough for him to have developed any deep feelings for them. BK was an overweight boy and says he remembers "feeling angry all the time." At age 13 he was introduced to marijuana and alcohol by older siblings and cousins, and began using both regularly. He was interested in school, but said he felt like an "oddball" because of his obesity and the fact that he was biracial.

BK describes his first serious interest in anything as his "enterprise" of mosh pit dancing. The mosh pit, an area near the concert stage in which metal, rock, or punk blares, provides a place for bodyslamming, stage diving, and crowd surfing. Bodyslamming is the activity of aggressively hitting one's upper body against another person in the pit. The object of bodyslamming is to express one's anger by making fierce physical contact without seriously injuring anyone. BK always wore old clothes so that he wouldn't mind too much if they were destroyed or soaked in beer. He had special shoes with hard tops and no laces. The point was not to dig in or shove or push, he said, but to use the palms of the hands. Stage diving is a riskier activity that involves jumping from the stage into the arms of the crowd. The crowd then carry the diver around the mosh pit, an activity called crowd surfing.

BK felt that the mosh pit provided a place for him to express his rage about feeling inadequate. He could go to the pit by himself and dance in the dark. He began to fear getting caught, however, since he was underage and had been using a fake ID. Although the substance of choice at the mosh pits is alcohol, BK said there were always drug dealers available who would try to make new contacts. Through a drug dealer he met at the mosh pit, he became aware of a variety of other drugs and decided to "experiment." He claims his motivation was to see if he could lose weight.

Later he came to realize that he was self-medicating his depression. He began getting high on cocaine and speed and was pleased to see that he actually did lose weight. With a slimmer body, BK wanted to try the rave scene.

A rave is a social event. It usually takes place in a dance club or other large open space. BK recalled that his mother had described to him the disco scene from her youth. He thought the rave might be similar: A large community of youth getting together late at night and dancing to a continuous mix of loud electronic music. In the background are colorful strobes and laser lights. Participants are dressed in colorful outfits and sometimes adorned with glow sticks. BK sold candies and sparkly jewelry at the raves that he would bring in his knapsack. He soon began to see how easy it was to sell drugs too. He made large amounts of money quickly. Rather than alcohol, BK and the crowd used drugs such as GHB, LSD, and ecstasy. The raves would last for hours. One morning around 8 am, BK was caught by the police as he was driving home after a rave with an array of drugs in his car. He received a four-year sentence.

Inmate JR

JR is a 21-year-old single Caucasian male. He is an only child. His parents divorced when he was 5, but they lived together off and on for several years. JR's father had been a drug addict who at times had been incarcerated for drug-related offences. JR recalled that he would do his best to keep his father and mother together, but at age 10 he was devastated to learn that his father was marrying someone else. His mother made matters worse by refusing to let him see his father anymore. She accused her husband of being just like his own father (JR's grandfather), "an addicted jail bum."

Stealing was the first "enterprise" that JR thought of when asked to describe his network of enterprise. He said that he began stealing from his school and church. He felt something was owed to him and he was going to get what he felt he was entitled to. Stealing cars became a game for him. The excitement of finding the right chop shop and getting the money made him feel that he had accomplished something. His biggest thrill was a successful attempt at eluding the police in a car chase at age 16. (This occurred even as he was on probation for a shoplifting charge.) He felt he had developed a skill.

JR's delinquent activities caused his mother to kick him out of their home. She asked his father to take him in. By this time JR's father had been in recovery for many years and was happy for the opportunity to help his son. But JR didn't quite trust the help. He complained that his father's new wife and children couldn't accept him and he ran away from their home. For months he lived with friends or in homeless shelters before his mother agreed to take him back into her home again. In spite of periods of hypomania and binge drinking, JR managed to graduate from high school. He saw a psychiatrist at his mother's insistence and was prescribed a mood stabilizer and diagnosed with Bipolar II disorder. He never took the medication and never went back to the psychiatrist, but instead began to use marijuana heavily.

JR had vague and unrealistic plans of starting his own business, and when his girlfriend became pregnant, he began to feel a sense of responsibility. Feelings of responsibility turned to fear and he became sexually promiscuous. He had a juvenile offense record, but he decided to see if he could get accepted into the military. Before that could happen, however, he ended up in a barroom brawl in which he seriously injured someone. He is now serving a five-year sentence for aggravated assault.

NETWORK OF ENTERPRISE

An enterprise is an enduring, purposeful activity consisting of projects and tasks and yielding products. It is possible to describe an enterprise as a discrete entity, although often enterprises overlap or branch into others. A creative person may organize many related tasks and projects in a network of different enterprises that provides continuity and meaning. An enterprise may lie dormant for a while and then be taken up again, but it rarely comes to an end; rather, it spawns new enterprises or generates new tasks and projects within the same enterprise.

To express the idea that this creative process is part of a self-generating system, Gruber (1980) provides the metaphor of Moses and the burning bush. The words, "And the bush was not consumed," is analogous to a creative system, which also does not come to rest when it has done good work or generated a product. A creative system also does not burn itself out in one great flash. "The creative life happens in a being who can continue to work" (p. 169). Enterprises are characterized by longevity and durability.

Is it possible to describe the broken lives of BK and JR in terms of failed networks of enterprise, and their projects and tasks as life destroying rather than life affirming? Inmates in the Life Review Group used the concept to formalize their life activities, both positive and negative.

BK characterized his young life by the following activities: mosh pit bodyslamming, stage diving, and crowd surfing; and drug and rave paraphernalia sales. These activities fall roughly within two enterprises, dancing and sales. Dancing for BK was less an art form than merely an outlet for his aggression. It never evolved. Similarly, selling drugs was a self-serving activity providing excitement. It required some cunning, but there was nothing extraordinary about it. His activities eventually died off (he outgrew mosh pits) or branched off into some other self-defeating activity (he went from the mosh pits to raves and drug sales). BK came to realize that the dancing, while legal, served no purpose other than to ventilate his own rage. His drug-selling work at the raves was illegal, in addition to harming those who bought from him.

The failure of stealing as an enterprise in JR's life became obvious to him before his decision to stop the activity. For a while, having a girlfriend seemed to provide some stability for him, but he was often careless and would not practice safe sex. His girlfriend's pregnancy was too stressful for him to handle. He acknowledges that "getting caught" provided the impetus for change and that the change was not self-generated. In his case, a system in chaos required an external pressure to right itself.

Amabile (1983) pointed out that the creative person is highly task-oriented and much less ego-oriented. People doing creative work are often characterized as selfish or autocratic, but usually this is understood as "necessary" for the work to be given the precedence it needs (it is difficult, demanding and long-term). The behaviors of BK and JR were primarily self-destructive. They struggled to identify themselves as worthwhile people, but in ways that brought nothing more than instant personal gratification (e.g., "fast money," having their sense of entitlement satisfied, or intoxication). Before incarceration, neither of these young men had attained a sense of self-identity, a pre-requisite to creating something beyond themselves.

BK and JR are now in healthier environments than they were before incarceration. They have both participated in anger management classes and 12-step programs to address addictions. They are becoming more aware of themselves and their vulnerabilities. Both know first-hand that there is no link between creative work and mental disorder, other than that they will need to do creative work to overcome their problems. They realize that any creative successes they may achieve will be in spite of their troubles and not because of them.

CONCLUSIONS

Experience in corrections has revealed that once deprived young men begin to explore their stories, they start to crave the kind of insight they discover. Lacking in traditional social skills and fairly immature in most ways, these inmates are eager to create their life narratives. Research indicates that in adolescence there is an emerging interest in biography. This is reflected in such behavior as keeping a diary or collecting material possessions as souvenirs of one's life. McAdams (1993) theorized that beginning in late adolescence and young adulthood, people construct more-or-less integrative narratives of the self in order to provide their lives with a semblance of unity and purpose. By reviewing early childhood experiences in the group setting, organizing single events into a coherent whole and exploring and examining old beliefs and views of the self, the individuals can begin to examine a variety of possible identities. The concept of network of enterprise can help to articulate this process. Incarceration for some is the life incident that triggers the need to create a life story, or search for meaning.

Formal operations enable the adolescent to reason hypothetically about his or her life, to relate the past and future to the present developing self. With thick description of incarcerated youth, psychologists can avoid rigid prescriptions of criminality or masculinity and see the ability of these young men to discover and change themselves. Research on mental health in prisons for men often focuses on the inmate's need to construct an armor, to establish a rigid masculine identity in order to survive (e.g., see Phillips, 2001). Thin description is based on generalities and assumptions that prisons are dangerous environments characterized by fear, deprivation, and subordination. It is true that there is certainly an aspect of paranoia in prison life, the need for a "trust no one" and "watch your back" mentality. However, the characterization of prison life as something that is dreaded and feared and in which one's manhood is cut down is different from that afforded by the thick description of some of the interactions in the Life Review Group.

The study of creative lives can be a model for the disenfranchised to become creative, to re-story their lives. Cognitive case studies of creative thinkers in the tradition of the evolving systems approach (e.g., see Wallace and Gruber, 1989), suggest that the formal operations stage is followed by a further diversification in which each creative individual pursues the development of a unique point of view. A point of view is necessarily influenced by one's level of privilege. The point of view of an impoverished, homeless adolescent is different from that of a more privileged youth. The former may have little respect for the idea of a point of view to begin with. Nevertheless, in prison, transition from a sense of apathy to a reverence for established rules is common. This points up that adolescents in prison are not taught to be creative, but are taught to follow rules. They can break the rules and will usually end up in Detention or Administrative Segregation status, or they can blindly follow the rules at the expense of stunting their identities. Indeed, the prime candidates for religious fanaticism in prisons are the inmates who feel most powerless. Rigid religious proscriptions can provide a stabilizing effect as well as a sense of identification. Teaching inmates to value their own narratives is the goal of the Life Review Group.

In his article "Creativity and Human Survival," Gruber (1989b) posed the question "How can anything one does make a difference?" His advice is:

> Take a developmental approach—start with what seems within grasp, then strive to expand the zone of the possible. Carve out a finite domain within which change can be detected, success identified. Try to define certain invariants, conditions that seem imperative, then look for flexible ways of maintaining these constants. There is probably no giant step that represents the solution, but very many one-percent steps, or even smaller. Choose a project and invent the steps that will be within your reach (pp. 285–286).

The evolving systems approach is developmental, phenomenological, and compatible with the techniques of narrative psychotherapy. Gruber provides a wealth of ideas for those who strive for change in the world. In the present case, his work was applied to the study of young incarcerated men for whom prison provides a haven from the chaos on the streets. If prisons are indeed becoming an alternative shelter for the mentally ill or for the economically disadvantaged, then mental health professionals have a venue to provide a valuable service to these inmates. The rise in the prison population also means that eventually there will be a rise in the population of released prisoners. Mental health workers need to provide an experience of growth for these inmates and to encourage self-exploration that can be continued after release from prison.

REFERENCES

Amabile, T.M. (1983). *The social psychology of* creativity. New York: Springer-Verlag.

Brower, R. (1999). Dangerous minds: Eminently creative people who spent time in jail. *Creativity Research Journal*. 12, 3–13.

Bruner, J. (1986). *Actual minds, possible worlds*. Cambridge, MA: Harvard University Press.

Butterfield, F. (2002, January 21). Tight budgets force states to reconsider crime and penalties. *The New York Times*, pp. A1, A11.

Chaiklin, H. (2001). Current and prior mental health treatment of jail inmates: The use of the jail as an alternative shelter. *Journal of Social Distress and the Homeless*, 10, 255–268.

Fine, R. (1973). A critical examination of the concept of acting-out in the neurosis of our time. In D.Milan, & G.Goldman (Eds.), *Acting out*. Springfield: Charles C. Thomas.

Geertz, C. (1973). *The interpretation of cultures*. New York: Basic Books.

Goffman, E. (1959). *The presentation of self in everyday life*. New York: Doubleday.

Gruber, H.E. (1989a). The evolving systems approach to creative work. In D.B. Wallace & H.E. Gruber (Eds.), *Creative people at work: Twelve cognitive case studies* (pp. 3–24). New York: Oxford University Press.

Gruber, H.E. (1989b). Creativity and human survival. In D.B. Wallace & H.E. Gruber (Eds.), *Creative people at work: Twelve cognitive case studies* (pp. 278–287). New York: Oxford University Press.

Gruber, H.E. (1980). "And the Bush Was Not Consumed": The evolving systems approach to creativity. In S. Modgil & C. Modgil (Eds.), *Towards a theory of psychological development* (pp. 269–299).Windsor, England: NFER Publishers.

Gruber, H.E. (1977). The study of individual creativity: A report on the growth of a paradigm with some excerpts from a little known document by the young Piaget. Paper presented at the Seventh Annual Symposium of the Jean Piaget Society, Philadelphia.

Gruber, H.E. & Davis, S. N. (1988). Inching our way up Mount Olympus:The evolving systems approach to creative thinking. In R. J. Sternberg (Ed.), *The nature of creativity*. Cambridge, MA: Cambridge University Press.

Harré, R. (1984). *Personal being*. Cambridge, MA: Harvard University Press.

James, W. (1890/1902). *The principles of psychology*. London: Macmillan. (Original work published in 1890)

Mazlow, A.H. (1968). *Toward a psychology of being*. (2nd ed.). Princeton: Van Nostrand.

McAdams, D.P. (1993). *The stories we live by: Peronal myths and the making of the self*. New York: Morrow.

Morgan, R.D., Winterowd, C.L., & Ferrell, S.W. (1999). A national survey of group psychotherapy services in correctional facilities. *Professional Psychology, Research and Practice, 30*, 600–606.

O'Hanlon, B. (1994). The third wave. *The Family Therapy Networker, 18–26, 28–29*.

Parry, A. & Doan, R.E. (1994). *Story revisions: Narrative therapy in the postmodern world*. New York: The Guilford Press.

Phillips, J. (2001). Cultural construction of manhood in prison. *Psychology of Men & Masculinity, 2*, 13–23.

Richards, J.M., Beal, W.E., Seagal, J.D., & Pennabaker, J.W. (2000). Effects of disclosure of traumatic events on illness behavior among psychiatric prison inmates. *Journal of Abnormal Psychology, 109*, 156–160.

Rorty, R. (1991). *Objectivity, relativism, and truth: Philosophical papers*.vol. 1. New York: Cambridge University Press.

Tahir, L. (1996). Growth through opposition: The development of a point of view in young Bernard Shaw. In M.L.Commons, J. Demick, & C. Goldberg (Eds.), *Clinical approaches to adult development* (pp. 29–53). Norwood, N.J.: Ablex Publishing Corporation.

Wallace, D.B. (1989). Studying the individual: The case study method and other genres. In D.B. Wallace & H.E. Gruber (Eds.), *Creative people at work: twelve cognitive case studies*. (pp. 25–43). New York: Oxford University Press.

Wallace, D.B. & Gruber, H.E. (Eds.). (1989). *Creative people at work: Twelve cognitive case studies* New York: Oxford University Press.

White, M. & Epston, D. (1990). *Narrative means to therapeutic ends*. New York: W.W. Norton & Co.

6

UNDERSTANDING EXTRAORDINARY MORAL BEHAVIOR IN CHILDREN AND ADOLESCENTS

Susan Rostan

He who would do good to another must do it in minute particulars.
General good is the plea of the scoundrel, hypocrite, and flatterer; for
art and science cannot exist but in minutely organized particulars.
William Blake

Gruber's (1993) concerns regarding the relationship between creativity and morality, voiced in the early part of the last decade, pulse with increasing intensity in our current struggles with terrorism. We as a nation have turned our attention to peoples and individuals who embody the need for fairness, justice, caring, and truth. These moral issues concerned Gruber years ago, but today they are on the minds of virtually all persons—those concerned with the absence of these moral behaviors as well as those concerned with their heroic presence.

In this chapter, I explore Gruber's theories regarding creativity and morality as a foundation for discussing theories of moral and extraordinary moral behavior in children. A review of the theoretical and research literature is followed by a discussion of teachers' beliefs and knowledge regarding moral and extraordinary moral behavior, and, in turn, by a summary of my collaboration with Rudnitski and Grisanti addressing extraordinary moral behavior in children, as seen through the eyes of their teachers. The findings of these explorations support Gruber's idea that moral creativity is the outcome of a discrepancy between what is and what could or should be. Moral action resolves this discrepancy.

DIFFERENTIATING PROSOCIAL BEHAVIOR AND ALTRUISM

Gruber (1987) observed that most discussions of moral development focus primarily on moral reasoning, and thus "neglect the topics of altruism, prosocial behavior, and moral responsibility" (p. 105). In fact, this lack of evidence relating moral reasoning with moral behavior notwithstanding (c.f., Blasi, 1980; Colby & Damon, 1992; Radke-Yarrow, Zahn-Waxler, & Chapman, 1983), conceptions of altruism and prosocial behavior are often conflicting and poorly constructed to begin with.

In the literature on children's altruistic behaviors, for instance, researchers distinguish between what is termed prosocial behavior– "helping" behavior—and altruism. Helping behavior is behavior that is either expected by others, or perceived as being needed by them to help them further their goals. Such behavior might include helping struggling students with their schoolwork or helping peers resolve conflicts through special programs. Psychologists, however, view many prosocial behaviors as motivated by factors such as the expectation of concrete rewards or social approval, or the desire to reduce one's own negative internal states (i.e., distress or guilt from observing a needy individual) (Eisenberg, 1992).

In much of the theoretical and research literature, furthermore, altruistic behavior, distinguished from helping behavior, is described as spontaneous and unexpected, self-initiated, and performed with no expectation of reward or praise (Bar-Tal, Raviv, & Leiser, 1980). Eisenberg (1992) described altruistic behaviors as prosocial behaviors motivated by sympathy for others or by the desire to adhere to internalized moral principles—suggesting that altruism is actually a higher form of prosocial behavior. Grisanti and Gruber (1999) further suggested that the identification of morality with the absence of all self-interest goes too far, reducing the concept of altruism to an unattainable state (e.g., Kohlberg's stages 5 and 6). From Grisanti's and Gruber's (1999) perspective, creative altruism engenders an active, "innovative expression of altruistic feeling and principle" (p. 427), with the degree of self-interest left unspecified. Far from an unattainable state, Gruber's conception invites us all to participate.

EXTRAORDINARY MORAL BEHAVIOR

Gruber (1987) elaborated on the common-sense use of the term altruism—which is unselfish concern for the welfare of others—noting that it implies an unsolved problem in the "distribution of resources" (p. 105). Gruber noted that an action taken eliminates the discrepancy between what is and what could be. Gruber (1993) clarified our understanding of creativity in the moral domain by describing it as behavior in situations lacking a clear means to moral action. When a bystander recognizes that something ought to be done, for example, action is taken only if something can clearly be done. Creative altruism, which we consider extraordinary moral behavior, emerges in situations lacking this clear means to action. Creativity thus plays a significant part in novel or challenging situations.

Gruber (1985) described a person exhibiting extraordinary moral responsibility as having high levels of moral reasoning, a concern for a society's important issues, strong moral passion, and the propensity and courage to translate thought and feeling into effective action. Creative altruism, according to Gruber, resembles other forms of creative work. Both require:

> Awareness of the possibility of something new, followed by the patient evolution of the understanding of the problem the translation of the inner life of desire and fantasy into forms of action in and upon the world ... prolonged, intentional search for adequate and harmonious solutions ... sensitivity to the impact of the innovation on some prospective audience or recipients. Especially in creative altruism, this takes the form of empathic awareness of the needs and feelings of the other (Gruber, 1985, p. 106).

According to Gruber, it is the self-chosen task of the creative altruist to work to provide his or her available resources to a recipient with an unmet need; the creative altruist's goal is to reduce or eliminate the discrepancy between what is and what could or should be. The cooperation of all participants in a helping situation is a key factor for Gruber; cooperation becomes part of the solution process as well as part of the goal.

Gruber's (1985) theory of extraordinary moral behavior involves: (1) taking moral initiatives; (2) living with the knowledge of a potential negative event or envisioning a need; (3) seeking an answer for the discrepancy between what is and what could be; and (4) taking positive, out-of-the-ordinary action. Berk (1989) noted that a good theory, beyond its elegance and aesthetic appeal, must guide our practical efforts to accomplish an important objective. Berk further noted that the importance of creating a good theory lies in its ability to tell us what to observe, how our observations are related, how to organize and make meaning from our research, and how to proceed rationally with practical actions. For all these reasons, Gruber's theory of creative altruism is an inspiring and effective theory. Rather than studying the typical development of moral behavior, Gruber's theoretical framework invites us to identify and understand unusual people who are in the process of developing extraordinarily responsible behavior—those who can and do take positive action.

THE EMERGENCE OF EXTRAORDINARY MORAL BEHAVIOR

Beyond noting the diverse and conflicting definitions of prosocial behavior and altruism, it is important to understand whether there are types or levels of altruistic behavior. Gilligan and Wiggins (1988), for instance, asserted that two moral injunctions—not to treat others unfairly and not to turn away someone in need—exemplify two lines of moral reasoning. The first injunction is based primarily on a state of inequality and the second primarily on caring and the ability not just to empathize with the feelings of others, but actually to feel what they feel—what Gilligan and Wiggins called co-feeling.

Co-feeling, according to these authors, differs from compassion; compassion connotes a state of feeling in which the compassionate person can empathize with the feelings of another who is in a less fortunate position. Co-feeling, on the other hand, implies a state of equality between two people; a deeper level of moral reasoning is thus implicit in a helper being able to feel what another feels, rather than merely to identify what another feels and help the other to feel better.

Co-feeling also differs from empathy. While empathy implies that self and other feel the same, co-feeling implies that an individual can actually experience feelings that are different from his or her own. Co-feeling is therefore participation in another's feelings, an engagement rather than a judgment or an observation.

Drawing from both Gruber's (1987) and Gilligan and Wiggin's (1988) conceptions of moral behavior, Rostan, Rudnitski, and Grisanti (1999; 2001) defined extraordinary moral behavior as involving action that brings about a change in the disposition of human resources, and reflects both a sensitivity to what ought to be done and a cooperative affective exchange with others. In other words, extraordinary moral behavior involves the ability to resolve a moral dilemma by seeing relationships in multiple ways—interweaving concerns about justice and concerns about care—and taking action that reflects both principles and co-feelings. Another view of moral behavior is that a hierarchy of behaviors exists in the development of moral agency.

As an integrationist, Rottschaefer (1998) worked to develop a scientifically based account of how we acquire moral agency and put it to work. Rottschaefer's model includes four functional levels: (1) a base level, comprising evolutionarily acquired and behaviorally learned capacities as well as tendencies to act morally in given situations; (2) a behavioral level, comprising a set of moral beliefs and desires driving actions, and being influenced by both base-level and higher-level components; (3) a reflective level, comprising higher-level beliefs and desires and including moral norms, and influencing the behavioral-level beliefs and desires; and (4) a self-referential level, comprising conceptions of the self and the self as moral agent, and mobilizing the use of moral norms and consequently moral action.

Rottschaefer does not suggest that for an action to be moral, it must engage all four levels of agency. His model includes a developmental theory of empathy, and Rottschaefer noted that empathy and sympathy often result in altruistic tendencies—prosocial actions that have the benefit of another as their object. One might infer that level-three behavior could encompass co-feeling actions and level-four behavior could be implicit in Gruber's conception of creative altruism. Research addressing rescuing victims, which follows, informs a discussion of the importance of specifying—in any discussion of extraordinary moral behavior—the degree of self-regard in actions and intentions.

RESEARCH ADDRESSING ALTRUISTIC BEHAVIOR: RESCUING VICTIMS

Many moral encounters involve victims or potential victims—persons harmed or made to suffer from an act, circumstance, agency, or condition. Oliner and Oliner's (1988) research, documenting the various characteristics of altruistic personalities—in this case the rescuers of Jewish victims of the Holocaust—points to the types, not levels, of behavior affecting the same humane results: altruism. Oliner and Oliner present an account of the relevant features of altruism in the actions of exemplary adults.

Oliner and Oliner's research suggests that, at the adult level, altruism may be a complex synthesis of behaviors—selfless and self-serving, rudimentary and abstract. When the two compare rescuers to nonrescuers—i.e., nonacting bystanders—they found that the two groups interpret the demands on themselves differently. Faced with the same knowledge, observation of needs, or requests, only the rescuers felt compelled to act.

Oliner and Oliner identified three kinds of catalysts for action: (1) empathically oriented rescuers—individuals who responded to an external event that aroused or heightened their empathy; (2) normocentrically oriented rescuers—individuals who responded to an external event which they interpreted as a "normative demand of a highly valued social group" (p. 188); (3) principled rescuers—individuals who behaved according to their own overarching and mainly autonomous principles and responded to an external event that they interpreted as violating these principles.

The rescuers' orientations, whether empathic, normocentric, or principled, were consistent with the ways rescuers characteristically made important life decisions. The orientations, further, were rarely found in a pure form in any individual case. Combinations of the three orientations and even concern with self-enhancing actions or fulfilling personal needs were apparent in some cases. Oliner and Oliner suggested that demonstrating competence to oneself in carrying out tasks and taking full responsibility for the results might have been motivating considerations for some rescuers.

The research also found that cues did not have to be visually obvious or forcefully conveyed to arouse an empathic response in the characteristically empathically oriented rescuers. Simply recognizing another's danger often prompted an empathic response, even when the victim made no explicit request for help. Oliner and Oliner found cases where empathy was a response to identification with contextual characteristics. They noted that in their research, perceived characteristics were sufficient to lead the rescuer to assume at least some time-limited responsibility for the victim's well-being. They concluded that understanding others, taking their perspective, being attached to them, and anticipating their possible futures may leave little room for one's own needs. This explanation of the characteristics of altruism moves it away from a larger concept of prosocial behavior, because of its overwhelming concentration on the status of others. However, Oliner and Oliner also found that a desire for praise, material goods, and in some cases, avoiding censure also contributed to some altruistic actions. More importantly, action was an extension of characteristic forms of relating to others. More often than not, it was typical behavior for the rescuers.

In the Oliner and Oliner research, those rescuers with principled orientations—rather than empathic or normocentric—most frequently exemplified two kinds of moral principles: the principle of justice and the principle of care (an obligation for helping the needy). Rescuers motivated by the principle of justice tended to have different feeling states from those of rescuers motivated by the principle of care. Justice-principle rescuers usually had more impersonal relationships with those they helped, and reserved strong emotions (anger and hate) for people violating the principle of justice they held dear. Care-principle rescuers, on the other hand, usually focused on the subjective states and reactions of the victims. Kindness toward the victim was a dominant theme, while hate and indignation toward the violators were more transitory.

Oliner and Oliner suggested that high independence from external opinions and evaluations was the major characteristic of people who shared this orientation of principled motivation. Unlike individuals with internalized norms—traced to authoritative social groups—the principled individuals appeared to develop through their own intellectual and moral efforts, clearly supporting Gruber's theory of the integral part that purposeful work plays in the evolving systems of extraordinary individuals. How these evolving systems—of knowledge, affect and purpose—emerge in children now becomes an important consideration for the scope of this chapter. One may find some answers in a theory of problem-focused coping skills (c.f., Moos & Schaeffer, 1988).

According to Moos and Schaeffer, individuals highly competent in problem-focused coping confront the reality of a crisis and its aftermath by dealing with tangible consequences, and by trying to construct a more satisfying situation. They seek information and support regarding the crisis, alternative courses of action, and probable outcomes. They also analyze the situation logically to try to restore a sense of control, thinking through steps and anticipating the potential demands that others might place on them. The final step—taking problem-solving action, which is a developed skill—can both draw upon and create a sense of competence and self-efficacy; the individual feeling some control is more likely to exhibit problem-solving coping strategies. Moos and Schaeffer concluded that caregivers who are mindful of issues in typical normative transitions and in prevalent crises within a culture can prepare individuals for these experiences, and thus help them expand their coping repertoires.

CHILDREN'S EXTRAORDINARY MORAL BEHAVIOR

Paley (1999) used the term "rescue" to describe a child's act of kindness toward another vulnerable child who has little or no skills in coping with a stressful situation. This perspective on rescue behavior provides a meaningful link between early manifestations of altruism in children and the self-reflecting, high-risk, & self-sacrificing acts of adults. Using teachers' narratives about children rescuing other children from suffering the pain of rejection and humiliation by peers, Paley revealed children's capacity for kindness. The narratives depicted teachers' sensitivity to evolving empathy, and to problem-focused coping skills in young children. Although Paley focused on the children's behavior, it is also important to consider not only what the narratives reveal about the teachers, but also the impact of socialization, as in a classroom situation, on a child's willingness to act altruistically.

Paley's research suggests that an essential aspect of understanding extraordinary moral behavior may be studying individuals who recognize this behavior in others (see below). When teachers witness their students' moral behavior, the actions that the teachers consider exceptional enlighten us about their own sensitivity as well as about the actions they consider creative. When a teacher actually witnesses a child taking action for the well-being of another child—with or without any apparent recognition or reward—he or she may characterize the behavior as kind, caring, or principled, and thus perhaps altruistic behavior. The teacher shapes his or her interpretations of the events in the school community to fit the form of existing understandings, or constructs a more appropriate understanding. Teachers then use these schemes to both assist and assess their students' performance.

Extending a bystander model to include the bystander of the bystander—a teacher observing a bystander taking action—empathic distress may be a reason for teachers' sensitivity to altruistic behavior and the motivation for identifying altruistic students. There may also be types and levels of moral behavior that teachers would characterize as extraordinary. These considerations invite an exploration of teachers' descriptions of their students' moral behavior.

UNDERSTANDING THE WITNESS: TEACHERS' CONCEPTIONS OF MORAL AND EXTRAORDINARY MORAL BEHAVIOR

In order to foster the development of moral behavior in their students, teachers must first understand the relevance and acquisition of such behavior, as well as the action exemplifying it. They can then make professional judgments and plan appropriate activities and programs. In a study of teachers' perceptions of children's extraordinary moral behavior my colleagues and I (Rostan, Rudnitski, & Grisanti, 1999; 2001), addressed the roots of teachers' beliefs and knowledge in this area. Assuming that teachers' beliefs and knowledge are central to their lesson plans—the "working capital of the professional" (Tilleman, 1995)—we reviewed literature concerned with how teachers construct informed understandings about moral behavior. We realized that to be measurably effective in identifying moral behavior in children as described by their teachers, researchers must understand teachers' perceptions and conceptions of that behavior in specific instances. We needed to know what, for the teacher, constituted spontaneous, observable extraordinary behavior in the children.

Demonstrably, teachers have beliefs about moral ends and justifications evolved from perceptions, memory, reflections, inferences, and norms as well as from such authorities as parents, other adults, peers, society, religion, and experts in the field. It is from these beliefs, modified by individual, social, and expert-assisted constructions, that teachers make judgments about their students' behavior and how to modify it. Relevant educational psychology typically focuses on exposing, and integrating theories of moral reasoning (e.g., Colby & Kohlberg, 1984; Gilligan & Wiggins, 1988; Kohlberg, 1971; Piaget, 1932), Selman's theory of perspective taking (e.g., Selman, 1980), and Eisenberg's theory of prosocial behavior (e.g., Eisenberg, 1992). My colleagues and I (Rostan, Rudnitski, & Grisanti, 1999, 2001) suggested that it is from personal beliefs and these various theories that teachers must construct their own professional understandings of the moral and prosocial characteristics of the children they teach.

At the same time, we noted that their understandings of moral action may be hampered by educational psychology's narrow focus on theories of the development of moral reasoning and by teachers' general lack of understanding of the topic as well. For example, theoretical and research literature suggests that the relationship between moral reasoning and moral behavior is a weak one, and that theories describing the development of moral reasoning do not provide a total understanding of how moral behavior develops. Radke-Yarrow, Zahn-Waxler, and Chapman's (1983) survey of the literature pointed out that variations in the frequency of prosocial behavior depended on the type of behavior, the ages of the children, and the research methods employed. The data simply did not allow any firm conclusions about the development of prosocial behavior before and during adolescence.

There is some evidence, however, that helping behavior increases in mid-elementary school, declines in late elementary or early high school, and then increases in high school. For example, Midlarsky and Hannah (1985), using interview data, found that children's fears of possible inadequacy often inhibit them from helping others. Midlarsky and Hannah also found that older preadolescents and young adolescents may be inhibited by a fear of social disapproval for helping (their help may not be wanted or it might embarrass the potential recipient) as well as by fear of being an incompetent helper. In summary, the Midlarsky and Hannah research suggests that older children tend to be more competent in helping because they have skills and experience that younger children lack.

Although older children have a larger repertoire of things they can do, however, the anticipated negative reactions of others may prevent some more competent older children from acting in helping ways.

A STUDY OF TEACHERS' PERCEPTIONS OF CHILDREN'S EXTRAORDINARY MORAL BEHAVIOR

A crucial feature of a narrative is that it can forge links between ordinary and exceptional behavior (Bruner, 1990). Bruner maintained that, while a culture contains a set of norms, it must also contain a set of interpretive procedures for understanding departures from those norms. In other words, we construct meanings of "extraordinariness" by beginning with the "ordinary." Departures from the expected behavior engender a search for "meaning" in the extraordinary. Rostan, Rudnitski, and Grisanti's (1999; 2001) study of teachers' perceptions of children's commendable moral actions explored highlighted memories of the extraordinary.

The research strategy was to analyze teachers' nominations for their school's humanitarian award. Participating teachers responded to a request to identify students exhibiting altruistic behavior during the school year. A committee of teachers evaluated the nominees and selected award winners based on the following criteria: the student made an outstanding effort in the school or community to help others, or the student was instrumental in starting a special program to help others. Nominees could satisfy either or both criteria. The same directives applied to students in the district's elementary schools, middle schools, and high school. Academic achievement, helping teachers, or merely being a good person were not qualifying behaviors. The cited behaviors reflected the teachers' own theories of extraordinary moral behavior and their need to share their observations.

The researchers assumed that teachers' narratives of these concrete, observable behaviors reflected their own values as well as the developing values of the children and adolescents. In spite of the limitations of assessing an individual's beliefs by analyzing descriptions of an event, the events clearly were real-life experiences for both the children and their witness, and the attempt was made to extrapolate from them what the witnesses typically valued in their daily experiences. The research question was: Do teachers' perceptions, depicted in narratives, reflect the definitions and manifestations of altruistic behavior in the theoretical and research literature?

The researchers analyzed 33 teachers' narratives, representing two consecutive years of award winners. The coded narratives identify the specific behaviors that the teachers categorized as worthy of recognition, as well as the context in which they took place.

Developmental Trends in Commendable Moral Behavior

The Rostan, Rudnitsky and Grisanti study (2001), suggested some meaningful trends and issues. For the study's elementary students, an overwhelming majority of witnessed behavior occurred in the classroom in interpersonal interactions. For middle-school students, the context of the behavior spread to include school programs. The context of the high-school students' witnessed behavior shifted to co-curricular programs (e.g., clubs and activities outside of the classroom), with little action in the classroom and little observed behavior in interpersonal activities. These contextual trends suggested a movement to more group and social contexts associated with age. The lack of witnessed behavior in interpersonal activities among high school students, however, does not mean there were none; it may simply reflect the changing opportunities teachers had for observing their students' interactions with others.

The context of the witnessed students' commendable moral behavior presented opportunities for action to which the students responded. The elementary students tended to take action in structured, supervised programs and activities and in workshops in which students could decide to help the teacher in response to his or her needs. These students also reacted to the emotional distress of others by providing quiet helping, taking on leadership roles, and, to some extent, performing in structured projects related to valued principles. The middle school students' actions tended to be in structured supervised programs and in situations offering opportunities to respond to a teacher's need. The high school students' responses were similar to those of the elementary students, but these older students were less inclined to participate in self-initiated quiet helping, take advantage of teaching opportunities, or respond to a teacher's need. The older students were more likely to take action in situations or structured projects related to principles or injustices. These trends suggested an age-related movement away from direct interaction with another individual in need, toward a more community-minded engagement in social action.

A majority of the elementary school teachers described their young students as acting as a teaching resource, and exhibiting sensitivity, caring and helping behavior, and volunteerism. With the exception of sensitivity and volunteerism, which decreased in the middle school students and returned in the high school students, the other characteristics (teaching resource, caring, helping) decreased with age.

Thus, our findings suggest some age-related changes in context, cues, and characteristic behavior. The study also revealed five issues concerning altruistic behavior in children, discussed below.

Conceptions of Altruism

In the context of a classroom or school community, the role teachers play as assessors—assigning grades for academic and social behavior–precludes their neutrality in the role of bystander. The study's discussion focused on whether the teachers believed helping behavior was altruistic.

In the literature on children's altruistic behaviors, as noted earlier, re-searchers distinguished between what is termed "helping" behavior and altruism. The teachers did not make, and could not reasonably be expected to make, these distinctions. Thus, for the purposes of this chapter, no distinction is made between the two terms. Indeed, although directives for a student's nomination explicitly noted that helping teachers was not an acceptable criterion for nomination, most of the elementary school teachers described situations in which a student was having difficulty with classroom work and another student intervened to help the teacher by helping the student in need. Taking advantage of teaching opportunities and helping by responding to teachers' needs was also evident, though to a lesser degree, in the middle school and high school narratives. It is clear from the narratives for all grades that the teachers valued this commendable behavior—helping them do their work.

One way of addressing the difference between a sensitivity to requests to help others and what Gruber's theory would describe as spontaneously providing one's available resources to a recipient with unmet needs, is to view requested help as a form of assisted performance—a scaffold generated to nurture future independent, spontaneous behavior. Using this perspective, we can look at how teachers' descriptions of behavior that we might consider "ordinary" moral behavior came to be thought of by them as commendable, extraordinary behavior. The limited nature of this commendable behavior suggests a relatively narrow repertoire of moral actions most young children can perform.

The Context of Moral Behavior

The study's second issue addresses the type of situation conducive to moral action. The context moved from the classroom and interpersonal relations in elementary schools, extending to school-wide programs in middle school, and almost exclusively to co-curricular programs and activities in high school. There was little evidence of individual sensitivity to principled behavior in the elementary school, although principles were inherent in structured programs. There was some evidence of individual sensitivity to principles in middle school situations, without mention of structured programs evincing the principles. Middle school students, unlike the elementary school students, did not tend to respond to teaching or leadership opportunities, but high school students did—suggesting the pattern of change that Midlarsky and Hannah (1985) found in age-related attitudes about helping others. On the one hand, the study by Rostan, Rudnitski, and Grisanti (1999, 2001) showed that, as they age, students become more aware of and empowered to act on principles of humane behavior to unknown others. Another way of expressing this would be to say that opportunities not noticed or thought to be impossible at a younger age now become possible. On the other hand, real-life altruistic actions— evident at an earlier age—may now be limited to friends, discounted by witnesses, or found irrelevant in the face of a broader, more community-minded perspective. The implication is that change is in the direction of what is relevant for the student and the community. Gruber's concept of a moral imperative may translate to "I can make a difference in the well-being and lives of others."

The Frequency of Extraordinary Behavior

Award winners fell into two categories: students who were always volunteering, always keeping the prosocial activities of their school community thriving; and students who performed dramatic, singular acts of caring. Teachers' narratives suggested that a child's moral activity could be witnessed in two forms: (a) as many small, continual acts of commitment and kindness that keep a community glued together; and (b) as big, infrequent acts of goodness.

Many, if not most, of the middle and high school teachers described behavior characteristic of good citizenship—contributing to the school community (e.g., volunteering for events, fundraising, etc.). Less often, teachers cited dramatic, almost heroic behaviors—commitments made to handicapped or dying children, for example. The dramatic acts were often recognized by the community at large—even written about in local papers. While teachers obviously recognized the singular, dramatic acts of altruism that a minority of students displayed, the most frequently reported behaviors were the many, perhaps otherwise invisible, equally important smaller contributions children made to the life of the school and community. Within the context of American middle-class life, the researchers suggested that serving the school community is an unheralded but nonetheless highly valued act. Such service may in fact be extremely important for children's and adolescents' integration into the mainstream of the school community. It is a context in which language, culture, and academic ability may pose less of a barrier.

Opportunity
Many of the big acts of kindness, caring, and compassion occurred in organized programs outside of the typical educational environment—in community programs, extracurricular clubs, and ESL classrooms. One can ask whether these unusual situations provide an important environment in which students are encouraged to develop an understanding of moral responsibility. It should be noted that the participating school district has a program aimed at getting students involved in community service. This is a required part of the curriculum in which high school students work in soup kitchens, hospitals, day care centers, and nursing homes. Even if community service is motivated by the need to meet a district's graduation requirement or to present a moral image to college administrators, the goal is to involve students in moral activities—experiences that facilitate an awareness of the needs of others and usually make students feel good about themselves. In other words, personal reward initially motivates the behavior that then becomes a satisfying and educational experience. The district's high school students are clearly encouraged to learn principles of moral behavior, take action, learn something about other members of their community, feel good about themselves, and understand the value of their actions to their community.

Grisanti and Gruber (1999) suggested that moral development and creative moral behavior can emerge suddenly as the result of both ordinary and extraordinary moral opportunities. This perspective is supported by Oliner and Oliner's (1988) research: people embedded in social networks favorable to altruistic activities are more likely to find more support for their efforts and may also be more likely to be asked by friends, relatives, or acquaintances to become involved in moral activities.

Thus, providing opportunities for students to use their knowledge to act, understand, and act again, in increasingly more personal and unique ways for the good of their community, is, perhaps, an achievable goal.

Extraordinary Moral Behavior
The fifth issue in the study (Rostan, Rudnitsky, & Grisanti, 1999, 2001), addresses the extraordinary nature of some children's moral behavior. We assumed that moral behavior could be precocious, creative, or spontaneous and unsolicited in school-aged children. We asked: Does it make sense to consider that some young people may have extraordinary moral ability?

In the teachers' narratives, the researchers found examples of Rottschaefer's (1998) conception of levels of moral behavior. Students of all ages, apparent stages of moral reasoning, and intellectual ability exhibited moral behavior at all levels of the typology. We noted that behavior at Rottschaefer's lowest level, i.e., instinctive everyday interactions among very young children, may be so common, so ordinary, that teachers did not think to offer examples of it in their narratives. The teachers did, however, offer examples of more advanced higher levels.

We found evidence of moral behavior that included some elements of Rottschaefer's level-two behavior—reasoning and reflections of social norms such as caring, kindness, and helping. However, teachers tended to identify as extraordinary those students exhibiting Rottschaefer's level 3 (reflective) and level 4 (self-reflective) behaviors, revealing their beliefs that they should act to benefit others. Such students may perhaps have exemplified desires fostered by the teachers, reflecting their valued norms and behavior.

Rottschaefer's level 4 behavior, reflecting the fulfillment of an individual student's potential, was also evident in some of the students: the students exhibiting both caring and principled action, i.e., they showed themselves to be empathetic, helping, responsible, independent, fair, and courageous individuals. In fact, teachers described the behavior of four elementary school students, one middle school student, and two high school students in these terms. In response to the question at hand, elementary school students revealed evidence of developing creative moral behavior in the idiosyncrasy of their actions. In further response to the question, extraordinary moral behavior, viewed as a movement toward action embodying Gruber's definition of extraordinary moral responsibility (Grisanti & Gruber, 1999), can indeed evolve from exceptional awareness and acceptance of moral challenge and an innovative, personal response to it. The teachers' recreated witnessed behaviors suggested an emerging theory of extraordinary moral behavior, and a basis for future validating research.

CONCLUSION

Any developmental scheme, such as the movement toward altruistic behavior presented and discussed here, implies a conception of the end state to which that development leads or could lead. At the adult level, altruism may be a complex synthesis of actions—selfless and self-serving, rudimentary and abstract. If one considers extraordinary development as Gruber (1989) has done in his notion of the organization of knowledge, affect, and purpose, we can envision multiple end states in which the potential for creative work focuses on unique altruistic performance generated when the repertoire of existing actions and understandings does not offer an adequate solution to an identified problem. Rostan, Rudnitsky, and Grisanti (1999, 2001) have pointed out that though the disposition toward low-level altruistic behavior may be innate, individuals who can be described as morally creative have developed their abilities to a more self-reflective, purposeful level. Thus, what may develop are not only the ability to empathize, or intentionally and automatically act or react, but also the ability and predilection to seek out opportunities that mobilize relevant skills and capacities, increasing sensitivity to both the witnessed and unwitnessed needs of others, in order to act. The study by Rostan and colleagues provided evidence that the emergence of extraordinary moral behavior can occur at a relatively early age and, perhaps with practice, evolve into a much-needed community-minded response.

The study of teachers' conceptions of students' extraordinary moral behavior suggests that moral activity develops in two ways: infrequent big acts of goodness that don't happen every day, and many small, continual acts of commitment and kindness that keep a community glued together. The implications for education may be found within the concept of problem-focused coping skills. The coping skills needed to deal with the many variations on the themes of loss and need may differentiate children who act as rescuers from those who can't act because they don't know what to do or don't know what they ought to do because they can't act. Moral and extraordinary moral behavior, as manifestations of coping skills, may reveal the meaning that goals have for an individual—in rescuing those who cannot act for themselves, for example—and the special processes used to achieve those goals. If extraordinary moral behavior is studied, the exploration should continue not in hypothetical situations or in contexts disconnected from children's actual thinking or doing, but in natural, real-life contexts. It is here that teachers can play the critical role as witnesses.

Beyond the role of witnesses, teachers may play an important part in the development of moral behavior. Teachers' unique understandings and coping strategies in problematic situations may be crucial to the development of their students' coping skills and capacities for moral behavior. These understandings determine how teachers make judgments and plan activities and programs in their attempts to foster the development of moral behavior. It is obvious that a teacher's perspective has a reflective and judgmental aspect to it—with typical moral behavior defining what is extraordinary and commendable. The teachers' judgments—reflecting beliefs, experiences, and knowledge—appear also to reflect their own levels of judgment, reasoning, and actions. These possibilities deserve further research. An essential aspect of recognizing extraordinary moral behavior may be the sensitivity to persons who value a moment's experience enough to bring themselves to act on it—to weave the connection between what is and what could be—in their own unique way. Recognizing moral and extraordinary behavior may be a fundamental prerequisite for moral and extraordinary moral action and for the ability to nurture this behavior in others. The Rostan, Rudnitsky, and Grisanti study (2001) leads us to an observation that is also an invitation. Rarely does an educational inquiry alone provide the impetus for a statement of value for cooperative behavior. Such an impetus typically requires a transforming experience before a community can explicitly value altruistic behavior. With the experiences of the tragic events of 9/11 and their aftermath, we as a larger community, have been transformed. As members of many communities, what we experience and act on affects not only who we are as teaches and others, but also as socially responsible individuals. Perhaps the first step in nurturing extraordinary moral behavior, perhaps even making the extraordinary ordinary, is to recognize, encourage, and celebrate ordinary decent behavior, especially in the minute particulars. That is our invitation.

REFERENCES

Bar-Tal, D., Raviv, A., & Leiser, T. (1980). The development of altruistic behavior: Empirical evidence. *Developmental Psychology*, 16 (5), 518–524.

Berk, L. E. (1989). *Child development*. Needham Heights, MA: Allyn and Bacon.

Blasi, A. (1980). Bridging moral cognition and moral action: A critical review of the literature. *Psychological Bulletin*, 88, 593–637.

Bruner, J. (1990). *Acts of meaning*. Cambridge, MA: Harvard University Press.

Colby, A., & Damon, W. (1992). *Some do care: Contemporary lives of moral commitment*. New York: Free Press.

Colby, A., & Kohlberg, L. (1984). Invariant sequence and internal consistency in moral judgment. *Monographs of the Society for Research in Child Development*, 48, (1–2, Serial No. 200).

Eisenberg, N. (1992). *The caring child*. Cambridge, MA: Harvard University Press.

Gilligan, C. F., & Wiggins, G. (1988). The origins of morality in early childhood relationships. In J. Kagan and S. Lamb (Eds.), *The emergence of morality in young children*. Chicago: University of Chicago Press.

Grisanti, M. L., & Gruber, H. E. (1999). Creativity in the moral domain. In Mark A. Runco & Steven R. Pritzker (Eds.), *Encyclopedia of creativity, Volume 1*, (427–432). San Diego: Academic Press.

Gruber, H. E. (1993). Creativity in the moral domain: Ought implies can implies create. *Creativity Research Journal*, 6, 3–15.

Gruber, H. E. (1989). The evolving systems approach to creative work. In D. B. Wallace & H. E. Gruber (Eds.), *Creative people at work: Twelve cognitive case studies*, (3–24). New York: Oxford University Press.

Gruber, H. E. (1987). Creative altruism, cooperation, and world peace. In T. J. Hurley II (Ed.), *The greater self: New frontiers in exceptional abilities research*, (103–118). Sausalito, CA: Institutes of Noetic Sciences.

Gruber, H. E. (1985). Giftedness and moral responsibility: Creative thinking and human survival. In F. D. Horowitz & M. O'Brien (Eds.), *The gifted and talented: Developmental perspectives*, (301–330). Washington, DC: The American Psychological Association.

Kohlberg, L. (1971). Stages of moral development as a basis for moral education. In C. M. Beck,

B. S. Crittenden, & E. V. Sullivan (Eds.), *Moral education: Interdisciplinary approaches*. New York: Newman Press.

Midlarsky, E. & Hannah, M. E. (1985). Competence, reticence, and helping by children and adolescents, *Developmental Psychology*, 21, 534–541.

Moos, R. H., & Schaefer, J. A. (1988). Life transitions and crises: A conceptual overview. In R. H. Moos (Ed.), *Coping with life crises: An integrated approach*, (3–27). New York: Plenum Press

Oliner, S. P., & Oliner, P. M. (1988). *The altruistic personality: Rescuers of Jews in Nazi Europe*. New York: Free Press.

Paley, V. G. (1999). *The kindness of children*. Cambridge, MA: Harvard University Press.

Piaget, J. (1932). *The moral judgment of the child*. New York: Harcourt Brace.

Radke-Yarrow, M., Zahn-Waxler, C., & Chapman, M. (1983). Children's prosocial dispositions and behavior. In E. M. Hetherington (Ed.), *Handbook of child psychology: Vol. 4. Socialization, personality, and social development*. New York: Wiley.

Rostan, S. M., Rudnitski, R., & Grisanti, M. L. (2001). Teachers' perceptions of extraordinary moral behavior. In N. Colangelo & S. Assouline (Eds.), *Talent development IV: Proceedings from the 1998 Henry B. and Jocelyn Wallace national research symposium on talent development*, pp. 425–428. Scottsdale, AZ: Great Potential Press, Inc.

Rostan, S. M., Rudnitski, R., & Grisanti, M. L. (1999). *Toward a theory of moral giftedness:Teachers' apperceptions of students' extraordinary moral behavior*. Paper presented at the annual meeting of the American Educational Research Association, Montreal, April.

Rottschaefer, W. A. (1998). *The biology and psychology of moral agency*. Cambridge, UK: Cambridge University Press.

Selman, R. L. (1980). *The growth of interpersonal understanding*. San Diego, CA: Academic Press.

Tilleman, H. H. (1995). Changing the professional knowledge and beliefs of teachers: A training study. *Learning and Instruction*, 3, 292–338.

7

CRITICAL EXPLORATION IN THE CLASSROOM
ITS PAST AND PRESENT

Yeh Hsueh

> Critical Exploration has two aspects: (1) developing a good project for the child to work on—developing a curriculum; and (2) succeeding in inviting the child to talk about her ideas—developing pedagogy: putting her at ease, being receptive to all answers; being neutral to the substance of the answer while being encouraging about the fact that the child is thinking and talking; getting the child to keep thinking about the problem, beyond the first thought that comes to her; getting her to take her thinking seriously.
>
> Eleanor Duckworth (2003)

The approach of Critical Exploration in the classroom, also known as teaching-research or extended clinical interviewing, is new to many people in education, even though it is rooted in a clinical tradition dating from the early 20th century. Nevertheless, a variety of clinical approaches that continue to abound in various shapes and forms are familiar to many. The "clinical method" is often applied to a wide range of curricular activities required in teacher education and special education programs. Although the topic here can be related to educational clinical variation, the purpose of this chapter is not to seek a possible affiliation to other clinical approaches, but rather to provide some background of Critical Exploration and to describe a number of principles that characterize the ideas embedded in this unique educational practice.

In this chapter, I first clarify and define the approach itself. This preliminary definition raises the question of how the approach developed over time, which I attempt to describe. The historical description inevitably invites a contemporary and practical question about how this approach will work in a classroom setting. Following an example from Duckworth teaching a poetry class, I discuss four basic principles of Critical Exploration that involve the issues of "opening the world" with all its complexity, developing collaboration, thriving on multiplicity and conducting research while doing Critical Exploration for learning and teaching.

WHAT IS CRITICAL EXPLORATION?

This approach is a learning-teaching-research activity in which students and the teacher are mutually engaged in exploring the world of the subject matter, and in which the teacher's learning is an essential part of her teaching and research.[1] "Activity" means active personal pursuit of a firsthand experience with objects to be studied. In this activity, students' direct contact with a concrete object is crucial, be the object a poem, a historical event, a mathematical function, a theoretical model, a plant, or a cow. The direct contact is meant to get students to interact with various aspects of the object with their hands, heads and hearts.

For example, when children visit a farm and learn to milk a cow, milking could allow rich connections with other aspects of children's own experience, e.g., with dairy products, with the concept of Pasteurization, or with cow's digestive system, and so on.

Keeping the contact with the object active and meaningful requires the teacher to make every effort to get students to grapple with the object in their own ways. In order to help students seriously pursue their own ideas, the teacher encourages them to explain what they have experienced with various aspects of the object by closely following, relating and provoking their explanations and reasoning. Often, the students' efforts to explain their understandings of the object further stimulate their own interest in the matter under study.

The activity also provides an opportunity for the teacher to learn. In addition to its usual connotation of the word "learning," the teacher's learning through Critical Exploration entails three levels of meaning:

---

[1] As a convenience, I use the pronoun "her" throughout this chapter when referring to teachers.

a. teacher's learning of students' knowing,
b. teacher's learning of her own understanding of the students' thinking,
c. teacher's learning as a way of conducting research of her own teaching.

This research level overlaps with the other two because, as mentioned at the outset, Critical Exploration in the classroom, also called teaching-research, engages students in thinking about specific subject matters, and follows the development of their ideas. By following how the students' ideas develop over time, the teacher actually conducts research on learning and teaching, and applies the findings of her research to her teaching. For example, Quintero (2001) worked with a group of third grade children in Puerto Rico over a dozen sessions to understand these children's understanding of local geography and of mapping. Delaney (2001) studied high school boys' developing understanding of the U.S. presidency by asking them what they noticed about photographs and articles, selected on the basis of their ideas. And Schneier (2001) worked daily for five weeks with a group of high school freshmen, helping them come to understand complexities of poetry.

Teaching-research is to be distinguished from both "research for teaching" and "teacher as researcher" in that there is no demarcation between the role of a teacher and that of a researcher. In this sense, it is like a clinical interviewing process in psychotherapy that requires the therapist to investigate the patient's thoughts in order to help the patient move forward in his life through his own actions. Like the therapist's work that often extends over time, teaching-research functions to understand students' learning over time (Duckworth, 1996). The second meaning in the case of the latter is its interactive feature that extends from the individual to the group. That is why this approach is also often called "extended clinical interviewing." Only in recent years has Duckworth applied the name "Critical Exploration" to her educational practice (Duckworth, 2003). Historically, this term and research practice is an extension of the empirical epistemology pioneered by Piaget and his colleagues.

HOW DID CRITICAL EXPLORATION EVOLVE?

An inquiry into the evolution of this educational practice inevitably leads to an examination of Jean Piaget's early scientific activities. In this section, I identify some historical evidence to outline the development of Critical Exploration.

As far as the genesis of this approach is concerned, it is helpful to examine the period after Piaget received his doctorate in science. He spent a year in Zurich between 1918 and 1919 in the hope of finding a psychological research method that would allow him to implement his philosophical studies. Piaget (1952a) attended the lectures of Carl Jung and Oskar Pfister, studied statistics and spent much time with Eugen Bleuler who was an expert on autism, which Bleuler believed was a tendency to rely on wish-fulfilling fantasies as a flight from objective reality. Bleuler's teachings made Piaget "sense the dangers of solitary meditation" (Piaget, 1952a, p. 244).

Piaget went to Paris in 1919 to work for Theodore Simon in the laboratory school of the late Alfred Binet, the best-known pioneer of intelligence testing. Simon gave Piaget both a task and a free-hand. The task was to standardize British psychologist Cyril Burt's intelligence tests by using them with the laboratory school children. In the morning, Piaget would go to the library to read or attend lectures at the Sorbonne (University of Paris) where Lèon Brunschvicg, a philosopher of science, in particular, "exerted a great influence on [him] because of his historical-critical method and his references to psychology" (Piaget, 1952a, p. 244). In the afternoon, he talked for long hours with children in the school who found "Monsieur Piaget's" questions quite amusing. While he engaged children in various long, free-flowing conversations, Piaget discovered the questioning patterns of psychiatric workers most helpful in revealing the reasoning processes that underlay the children's answers.

This was the beginning of what was later called Piaget's "clinical method," and was the beginning of his experimental era even though, at the time, the method had no name. A strong psychoanalytical vein was evident in Piaget's method which he finally brought into being in Paris. And yet this vein cannot be credited as the formative influence in Piaget's method. There were more important ideas behind the method than psychoanalytical ones.

An important fact that has often escaped critics of Piaget's work is the profound influence of Brunschvicg's teaching on him which, in my view, was the engine that drove him to borrow from psychiatric procedures. According to Piaget, two aspects of Brunschvicg's influence were crucial. One was the previously mentioned historical-critical method that focuses on the mechanism and instruments through which earlier ideas and reasoning influence the formation of subsequent ones (Piaget & Garcia, 1989).[2] The second influence of Brunschwicg was the belief that the active

---

[2] In their studies of creative people at work, Gruber and Wallace (2001) described this intellectual development as the Network of Enterprise—a continuous flow of idea development

exchange of ideas is essential to scientific work. Any scientific objectivity can be achieved only through collaborative work—understanding, verifying and improving each other's ideas (as exemplified in Piaget, 1995, 1966, 1965, 1929). The research method that he and his colleagues used to investigate children's thinking embodied this view and so did his theoretical work.

In 1921, Piaget joined the Jean-Jacques Rousseau Institute where he soon drew up a plan to do a series of four books exploring child logic (Gruber & Vonèche, 1995).[3] In those days, Piaget taught and led his students to do research in la maison des petits (the House of Little Children) which was both part of the Institute and a public elementary school in Geneva. Édouard Claparède (1925), Director of the Institute, introduced the Institute to the U.S. audience, and described Piaget's investigation of children's logical thinking as "clinical examination" (p. 94). By the time Claparède made this comment, Piaget was writing *The child's conception of the world* in which, for the first time, he delineated his "method of clinical examination" and specified the rules and criteria for diagnosing and interpreting children's verbal responses. He made it clear that this method of clinical examination was analogous to the method employed by psychiatrists as a means of evaluation:

> For example, one may for months examine certain cases of paranoia without once seeing the idea of grandeur assert itself, though the impression of it is behind every unusual reaction. Moreover, though there are not differentiated tests for every type of morbid condition, yet the practitioner is able both to talk freely with the patient whilst watching carefully for evidence of morbid obsession . . . naturally without knowing exactly where the obsession may suddenly crop up, but constantly maintaining the conversation on fertile soil (Piaget, 1929, p. 7).

This analogy suggests that the actual clinical examination sustains a relationship with another person, be it a child or a psychiatric patient, over a long period of time, with searching attention and strenuous effort given to following that person's thought. The practitioner was

that, from time to time, may branch out to form new enterprises or fuse with already existing ones. The result is a web of co-existing and sequential enterprises that at any given point represents the purpose of the person at that point. The enterprises can be active or dormant at different phases of development while significantly or potentially being connected with one another. Piaget's lifelong research activities demonstrated this evolving network of enterprise.

[3] These four books are: *The language and thought of the child* (1923); *The judgment and reasoning of the child* (1924); *The child's conception of the world* (1926); and *The child's conception of physical causality* (1927). See also a recent review of Piaget's method by Mayer (2003).

responsible for providing a continuous and enriching range of topics that could reveal, in the conversation, the thinking process of the person. By purposefully pursuing this process, the practitioner conducted an experiment:

> This clinical examination is thus experimental in the sense that the practitioner sets himself a problem, makes hypotheses, adapts the conditions to them and finally controls each hypothesis by testing it against the reactions he stimulates in conversation. But the clinical examination is also dependent on direct observation, in the sense that the good practitioner lets himself be led, though always in control, and takes account of the whole of the mental context, instead of being the victim of "systematic error" as so often happens to the pure experimenter (Piaget, 1929, p. 8).

In this passage, the dual quality of experiment and direct observation in one process was probably the most striking dialectical feature of the clinical examination. Conceived as an on-going process, this method sets itself apart from other research methods in that it seeks and preserves every response from the child in its living context. "The context may be one of reflection or of spontaneous belief, of play or of prattle, of effort and interest or of fatigue" (Piaget, 1929, p. 10).

In 1933, on the occasion of giving a talk to history teachers at an international conference, Piaget (1933) introduced the "clinical method" to teachers. First, he pointed out the deficiencies of preset questions in the questionnaire method that was popular at the time with both teachers and psychologists who studied children. Then he turned to the method he and his students used in Geneva:

> Therefore, little by little, the questionnaire method is being superceded by the direct questioning of the child, in a free and easy conversational form. This may be called the "clinical method". It is sure and has given converging results, but it is laborious, slow and difficult, like any other scientific analysis (Piaget, 1933, p. 17).

The last sentence is characteristic of descriptions of the clinical method. Furthermore, this scientific method was being introduced to history teachers! The laborious, slow and difficult process, according to Piaget, was important to teaching history because it was meant for studying "the child's spontaneous intellectual attitudes" (Piaget, 1933, p. 18) toward the historical event and its relation to the present, the subject matter that children needed to learn. As a scientific analysis, this clinical method carried a broader meaning than the usual hypothesis-testing and empirical verification. Piaget seemed to see in his research method a potential value for teaching history in the classroom.

But in the 1930s, a major watershed was apparent in his method of clinical examination. In an interview with Richard Evans (1973) who asked Piaget what he did wrong in his early work, Piaget replied, "Oh, my errors. I believed in language too much. I had the children talk instead of experiment...I wasn't sensitive to that. It wasn't until I had my own children and saw what they did before language..." (Evans, 1973, p. 70). This was not the first confession from Piaget. The arrival of his children in the late 1920s piqued his interest in pedagogy (Piaget, 1952a). In 1953, he remarked that, "it was essential to go back to the actions themselves, to the reasoning which is carried out not through language but through manipulation of objects. Starting with my books on the first and second years of child development my technique has always been to study reasoning through objects set up so that the child could make certain experiments" (Tanner & Inhelder, 1956, p. 32). The watershed was revealed in the new empirical experimental method in Piaget's books. The first of these books that he referred to is *The origins of intelligence in children* (1936/1952b) which first appeared in English in 1952. Almost 70 years later, this book is still considered by developmental psychologists in the English speaking world as "the Number One most revolutionary study since 1950" (Dixon, 2002, p. 4).

Researchers such as Gallagher and Reid (1981), Ginsburg and Opper (1979), Gruber and Vonèche (1995), and Inhelder, Sinclair and Bovet (1974), have noted this significant emphasis on action, a modification of the early clinical method. Ginsburg and Opper (1979) also coined the term the revised clinical method. After concluding his infancy study in the mid-1940s, Piaget stopped interviewing children, a research activity he had pursued for almost thirty years. Bärbel Inhelder who, some American social scientists in the 1950s believed, would soon succeed Piaget (Hsueh, 1998), became responsible for training students and researchers. About this time, Piaget took to using the term critical method, rather than clinical method (Bang, 1988, p. 40), partly derived from Brunschvicg's historical critical method. The alternating use of "critical" and "clinical" continued until the 1970s when Inhelder and her colleagues combined the "clinical method" with experimentation through a longitudinal design, and explicitly brought forth the method of critical exploration (Inhelder, Sinclair & Bovet, 1974, pp. 18–24).

"Clinical" maintains the sense of continuous, descriptive and reflective qualities; but "critical" adds the idea of the empirical experiment which involves the objective world. The idea requires "a more directive experimental method" because the purpose of this method is to provide children with optimal opportunities for interaction, both with the physical environment and with the experimenter (Inhelder, Sinclair & Bovet, 1974, p. 24). In

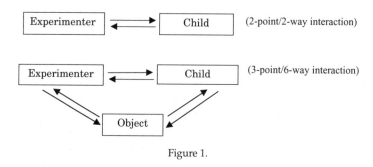

Figure 1.

fact, the "critical exploration" was an outgrowth of "clinical examination." The word "clinical" was initially a deliberate choice to set Piaget's method apart from testing or questionnaire methods that were common in the 1920s and beyond (Bang, 1998; Piaget, 1933). "Clinical" also acknowledged the psychoanalytical tradition (Piaget, 1929), empathetic listening to what the child had to say, and careful examination of how the child's earlier thoughts and feelings shaped current ones. This characteristic ran against the pre-scribed questions in the questionnaire method. The watershed in Piaget's method—shifting from the "clinical" to the "critical"—de-emphasized ver-bal interaction as the single most important means by which to look into children's thinking. "Critical" conveys a meaning which the commonplace "clinical method" often lacks, namely, the experimental adventure.

The method of critical exploration, proposed in the 1970s, invited par-ticipants to tell their beliefs, arguments, and reasoning through acting on objects, or the physical environment, and interacting with the inter-viewer/experimenter. This emphasis added a third interactive point to the earlier two-point/two-way interaction between interviewer and intervie-wee in the clinical method: the physical environment made the interaction three points and six ways. It also projected an educational possibility be-cause the experimenter, like a teacher, was involved in the child's learning.

This methodological concept, articulated by Inhelder, Sinclair and Bovet (1974), embodied a dual focus: on development and on exploratory actions through experimental adventures. It has informed the present dis-cussion of a pedagogical derivation in education: the approach of Critical Exploration in the classroom.

The use of the term, "approach" instead of "method" widens the ap-plication of "critical exploration" in a variety of learning and teaching con-texts, in which participants act on things rather than only talking about things. This interactionist position was held firmly by Piaget, and is a key idea in Eleanor Duckworth's work with teachers (Duckworth, 1997, 2001). She valued two main inspirations for her career in studying teacher education: Piaget's work and her own experience with Elementary Science Studies, a group of science curriculum developers in the 1960s (Duckworth, 1996).

Duckworth studied with Piaget in the late 1950s and served as his interpreter when he toured and lectured in the United States during the last fifteen years of his life. But for her thorough grasp of the method, Duckworth credited Bärbel Inhelder "at whose side and through whose patience I learned, among other things, the practice of clinical interviewing" (Duckworth, 1996, p. ix). Inhelder (1989) recalled that, in the 1960s, she began introducing her students to a method that combined two orientations:

> one where the researcher studies individual subjects keeping in mind a theoretical problem of genetic epistemology and psychology, and one where the psychologist or psychiatrist studies an individual human being in order to understand his or her specific potentialities and difficulties. (p. 233)

These two orientations, in retrospect, not only revitalized the early methodological insights, but also initiated a varied method called for by new problems regarding the relationship between learning and the development of cognition. They pointed in a direction of research that Piaget, except in his infancy research, had not always been interested in doing: studying individuals' learning over time (Duckworth, 2001, p. 186; Gruber & Wallace, 1999, p. 97). But this was Inhelder's long-time interest, witness especially her longitudinal studies (Hsueh, 1998). In a series of studies, Inhelder, Sinclair and Bovet (1974) refined the clinical method to allow quasi-naturalistic observations of behavior with a paradoxical emphasis: helping children think differently without telling them what to think, which amounts to a novel aspect of critical exploration.

In a similar vein, Duckworth made further methodological advances suitable for teacher education, one that takes account of individuals' learning in a group. This approach deals with learning, teaching and research through the teacher's and students' involvement in shared activities over time. As she moved from psychology to teaching, Duckworth noticed how her interviewing process concurrently helped to pique learners' interests, seize their attention and spur them on to further learning. This insight arose from the effort to help learners take their own thinking seriously, pursue their own questions, and wrestle with their own confusions while the teacher actually conducted research on their developing ideas (Duckworth, 1996). The approach stimulates learning activities without spelling out exactly what the learner should do. For two decades, she and her colleagues have documented diverse experiences of teaching-research in classrooms

(Duckworth, 1986, 1987, 1996, 1997, 2001; Duckworth, Julyan & Rowe, 1985; Julyan & Duckworth, 1996).

Critical Exploration is different from its forerunners in psychology because it is grounded in extensive work with teachers, children, and different kinds of adult learners in a variety of subject areas. Unlike any experiments in the psychological laboratory, the participants are learners in school and in everyday life. The teacher seeks an understanding that will be helpful to them. In this sense, Critical Exploration is also to be distinguished from most educational research that is conducted by those who are not responsible for teaching a subject or developing a curriculum in schools.

FOUR PRINCIPLES OF CRITICAL EXPLORATION IN THE CLASSROOM

Critical Exploration is itself a teaching and learning process. It may be helpful first to quote an example from Duckworth (1996) and then discuss its basic assumptions. This example happens to be about exploring a poem, but—as Duckworth pointed out later—people establish access to poems in multiple ways just they do in science.

> When studying a poem with a class, I start by asking students what they notice—an invitation to keep every complexity of the poem under consideration. People notice very different things, and almost every thing noticed leads to a question or another thought. Putting together what everyone notices and returning to the poem to try to look for answers to the questions leads to an understanding of the poem that is greatly expanded for each of us. Take, for instance, this Frost poem:

> Design

>> I found a dimpled spider, fat and white,
>> On a white heal-all, holding up a moth
>> Like a white piece of rigid satin cloth—
>> Assorted characters of death and blight
>> Mixed ready to begin the morning right,
>> Like the ingredients of a witches' broth—
>> A snow-drop spider, a flower like froth,
>> And dead wings carried like a paper kite.
>> What had that flower to do with being white,
>> The wayside blue and innocent heal-all?
>> What brought the kindred spider to that height,
>> Then steered the white moth thither in the night?
>> What but design of darkness to appall?—
>> If design govern in a thing so small.
>>   (Frost, 1969, p. 302)

Somebody will notice that there is a lot of white. Somebody will mention the rhyme scheme, or will imitate the rhythm. Somebody will mention that the first part of the poem seems to present a picture, and the second half seems to ask questions about it. Different people point out different possible plays on words: kindred and dreadful kin; appall and a funeral pall; a paper kite and a bird kite; morning right and morning rite; morning and mourning. Different people have different thoughts about whether the darkness is that which appalls, or that which is appalled.

Arguments develop about why the flower is described as white in the first line, and blue in the ninth. This is a bare beginning. A group of adults can easily go on for more than an hour with increasing interest and everybody's initial understanding is expanded by hearing from others.

I have always been frightened by being asked: "What is the meaning of this poem?" My reaction is, "How could I know? I'm no good with poems!" But it is easy for me to point out something that I notice about it. And in turn to listen to what other people notice about it, and to figure out whether I think that what they say makes sense, and why, and what other thoughts their ideas provoke in me. Many students have feelings similar to these. One in particular said that she had determined when we started discussing the poem that she would not say a word, knowing nothing about poems and feeling scared by them. But as she heard the various things that people were saying, her own thoughts developed, and she finally couldn't contain herself, so much did she have to say and so strongly did she feel about it. One student referred to himself as a "poem-phobe," which prompted another student to say, "If Frost had been able to put what he had to say into a sentence, he would have. So don't worry that you can't."

I recognized that this was the same thought I had about the accessibility of science. It is in acknowledging the complexity of the poem, not "sanding away at the interesting edges," to use Schneier's (1990) words, that we render it accessible. Our understanding seeks to do justice to the complexity that the poet sought to render, and by the same token it belongs to us. Just as the poet seeks to present his thoughts and feelings in all their complexity, and in so doing opens a multiplicity of paths into his meaning, likewise a teacher who presents a subject matter in all its complexity makes it more accessible by opening a multiplicity of paths into it" (Duckworth, 1996, pp. 130–131).

This excerpt consists of, and demonstrates, four distinct assumptions or principles of Critical Exploration: The key is to open up part of the world and make it accessible to learners; learning is an individual effort through collaboration; complex phenomena in the world engage the mind in learning; and finally, understanding the learner's understanding is itself a research finding that is fed back into teaching. These four principles, all emphasizing the developing nature of learning, are discussed separately below.

Opening the World vs. Opening the Mind

For many clinical methods, the focus is on language that is simultaneously a vehicle, a tool and an object. However, Critical Exploration introduces materials into the interview which the participants then can act on. The introduction of objects alters the features of classic psychotherapy, including play therapy that uses objects such as toys or dolls to diagnose fixations and developmental deficiencies. In Critical Exploration, materials are used as the subject matter of study. The key is to make the object accessible to people while keeping the complex relationships the object contains intact. To ask people what they noticed embodies this key idea. As shown in the example of teaching the poem, the principle is to "open the world" of poetry by providing simple access to this world without simplifying it.

Introducing an object like the poem through the approach of Critical Exploration creates multiple paths into the poem, and opens up a world of possibilities for learners to experience and learn the poem. As the example shows, everyone has something to convey about the poem. This feature shares a similar root both in the work of Piaget's team and that of some science educators who, with or without Piaget's influence, ask learners to act on objects and then follow their thinking. And yet, in Critical Exploration, it is "opening the world" (Duckworth, 1990) that stands out, as opposed to the widespread popular message, to "open minds," and "rouse minds." Opening up the world means bringing to learners a world of possibilities for them to get engaged with, creating their own connections and following their own meaningful paths. The world is full of possibilities for the mind to explore. The teacher engages students with the habits and peculiarities of the world such as the waxing and waning of the moon, or in the case of the poem, the images, the rhyme, the colors, the relations between different lines and stanzas. To open the world is to enrich the possibilities for the mind to be active and aware of a variety of relationships through its contact with all the possibilities.

David Hawkins (1967) described the world-opening aspect of teaching as focusing on "it"—a subject matter that both teacher and students can share, explore and maintain in continuous learning (e.g., new questions, new connections, new awareness of one's past understanding, and how others' understanding is related to one's own). In Critical Exploration, there must be a sharing of "it" between teacher and students and among the students themselves; in this way, they can follow each other's ideas by sharing the same references to the phenomenon. In the sharing, the collaborative work is both intellectual and moral. By "Intellectual," I mean the person's desire and mind's work to grasp the phenomenon at issue and the intricate relationships it presents; by "moral," I mean each participant's respect for the ideas of others in every possible way. This process leads to the next principle.

Collective and Collaborative Endeavor

As already mentioned, Critical Exploration is fundamentally a collective and collaborative endeavor, both from a historical perspective and in its present development and practice. Let us recall Brunschvicg's two principles which Piaget followed in his work: (1) that the historical-critical method focuses on the transformation of early ideas and reasoning and their influences on the formation of those that follow; and (2) that scientific objectivity cannot be achieved without collaborative work in understanding, verifying and improving each other's reasoning. Both these principles are as essential and evident in Critical Exploration as they were in Piaget's life-long research. Between these principles—transformation and collaboration—lie the influence and incorporation of ideas that take place in the process. One person's ideas can be instrumental in influencing the formation or transformation of one's own later ideas, or those of others. To understand the effect of this kind of influence in learning, the teacher uses Critical Exploration in order to follow closely how the early ideas develop into the later ones in one person as well as in a group.

In the process of noticing something in Frost's poem, the students, including self-proclaimed "poem-phobes," began to see phenomena emerging from the poem. But the increase of notable phenomena, not apparent at the outset, evolved through contributions from many individuals. The diverse observations made by the learners of the poem demonstrated a natural collaboration; and their feelings, including those of the teacher, toward the poem changed through this collaboration and moved the participants' thinking forward. They cannot but look at each other as learners whose thoughts, feelings, confusions and insights intersect with one another (see also Duckworth, 1990).

Throughout the critical exploration activity like the poem session, there is always an emphasis on maintaining harmonious relationships among all the participants even though the teacher is more focused on the flow of students' ideas and their interactions, while the students are more focused on the object of study. A harmonious dynamic cannot be sustained without mutual respect among the participants. New ideas cannot be advanced without each person seriously valuing his or her own ideas as well as those of others. Moreover, only through this kind of group work do people further develop their respect for each other's human intellectual integrity and the relativity of scientific objectivity as Duckworth noted earlier. Critical Exploration embodies an endeavor to balance and benefit the group and the individual, so that neither is emphasized at the cost of the other. This effort is hard to conceptualize, and even harder to practice. But it exemplifies a central principle of Critical Exploration—always to keep the complexity in view.

Keeping "It" Complex

Keeping "it" complex is fundamentally an epistemological issue. Since the beginning of universal schooling in many countries, particularly at the elementary and secondary levels, prescribed curricula have not given much attention to how children learn in particular or how people learn in general. Although the diverse expressions of the progressive movement in the first part of the 20th century made remarkable forays into elementary schools, and its influence continues to be present in early education (Nager & Shapiro, 2000), its momentum has not been a constant through the rapid societal changes. As a result, how people come to learn something in school is decided more by an authority which sets up the curriculum rather than by those who try to teach and learn.

Critical Exploration exemplifies one significant effort to restore the balance by studying teaching and learning with people directly involved. This effort may not be new on the surface because "student-centered," "cooperative learning" and "community of learning" all seem to present a similar flavor. Idiosyncratic to the Critical Exploration approach, however, is its principle of keeping "it"—the subject matter—complex through the efforts of both the teacher and students. In exploring the Frost poem, the complexity of the subject matter first came from the intricacy of the poem and then it became palpable and intriguing as participants began noticing more and more phenomena. Thus, the principle of emphasizing complexity is after all an acknowledgement of people's multiple ways of knowing. "It" is complex because people's needs and experiences are complex, thus the ways in which they grapple with "it."

The teacher's teaching is correspondingly complex because her teaching is part of the learning and research. A modified chart (see below) may illustrate this point by showing the six-way interactions. For the teacher, the continuous interactions including those involving her as shown by the arrows can be more than six ways. She will study the learner's effort to understand the object, and the interaction between them (3). At the same time, she will closely observe the other interactions (1) and (2).

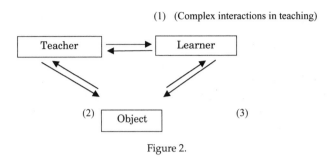

Figure 2.

Critical Exploration is also to be distinguished from discovery learning and conventional teaching in that it treats teaching and learning as a unity, and as a constantly changing process through interaction. Teaching improves with the teacher's participation in her students' thinking processes, and reflections on their active hand-head-heart involvement in learning; and learning progresses through the teacher's learning of her students' experience with the subject matter, with their own thinking, with one another, and with her teaching. Therefore, it is not an act of discovering what is out there in the reality, but a process of developing ideas that proceed slowly with increasing complexity through different ways of knowing.

Although Piaget did not plunge into any concrete educational research, his long-time interest nevertheless led him to this insightful comment about future education: "It seems clear that the future of the teaching of the sciences will depend more and more on their epistemology, something of which there are already many indications" (Piaget, 1976, p. 27). Today, decades later, looking at the acceleration of various constructivist teaching movements since 1973 (Hsueh, 1994), we may find it hard to disagree with him, and also add that his vision proves to have gone beyond the teaching of science. There is no question that discourse about constructivism in education is rightly about epistemology (see Ariasian & Walsh, 1997; Hawkins, 1994; Reid, Kurkjian & Carruthers, 1994; Tobin, Tippins & Gallard, 1993; von Glasersfeld, 1995). Learning from the world can be infinitely complex. This complexity provides ample resources for people to develop their own ideas about various relationships through their own ways of knowing. To help people develop their ideas, the teacher not only needs to find curriculum materials like the Frost poem that lend themselves to maintaining the complexity of learning activities, but also needs to understand students' learning in order to facilitate it. In this sense, a main part of Critical Exploration is research.

Teaching–Research

Teaching-Research, another name for Critical Exploration in the classroom, can be distinguished from various kinds of research of and for teaching. Teaching-research activity is similar to Piaget's clinical examination and his colleagues' method in that it is both experimental and observational. In a learning and teaching scenario, the teacher presents a problem, makes guesses, explores them and evaluates each guess by testing it against the reactions through her own participation in the shared activity. It is a deliberate and critical endeavor to understand learners' understandings, by researching learners' thinking as if she were Piaget at work (Duckworth, 1996, pp. 83–97).

To be sure, the use of teaching-research in the classroom has a different goal from Piaget's research program: Teaching-research is to understand the learner's understanding for the purpose of getting the learner engaged in further learning. This purpose mandates another unconventional practice in research: applying the findings to the students' learning activity as soon as they arise. In other words, the teacher's research findings are applied to the current activities the learner is engaged in. This direct and immediate application (not merely explanation or implication) of research findings distinguishes Critical Exploration from the widely accepted research in education that relies on third-party inquirers to examine learning and teaching from the outsider's point of view.

Conventional inquiry in the social sciences values the outsider's objectivity in the belief that it can offer explanation, rather than description. However, advocates for humanistic or phenomenological research argue that the researcher and the participant are inseparable. Since the research is a meaning-making process, the phenomenologically-inclined researcher values descriptions from the research participants (Giorgi, 1985), instead of the researchers' self-report as explanation. Thus, it may be argued that phenomenological research with its close examination and interpretation of the real "life-world" (Becker, 1986; Osborne, 1990; Polkinghorne, 1989, 1994) is philosophically akin to Critical Exploration in education. The teacher can explore two kinds of thinking simultaneously: that of others and her own. By exploring other people's thinking in interaction with objects, she examines and adjusts her own exploration, her examination of the learning process. The last two paragraphs in the above excerpt from Duckworth show how the teacher relates her own learning and thinking to the students' learning and thinking.

And yet, three differences in teaching-research also stand out from these phenomenological approaches. First, with its direct application, teaching-research distinguishes itself from phenomenological research in that it is not just to learn and understand participants' understandings and to report an accurate and insightful description. Rather, the findings are applied immediately or later to further the participants' learning. Second, therefore, learning, teaching, and research are intertwined in one unified activity that not only aims at developing the participants' knowledge, but also facilitates the development of a meaningful and interesting curriculum to advance multiple ways of learning from participants' points of view. Third, to achieve these goals, the teacher makes strenuous efforts to study both personal and collective learning over an extended period of time. This is why teaching-research, synonymous with Critical Exploration, has also been called extended clinical interviewing (Duckworth, 1996).

CLOSING REMARKS

No matter what names we have used for this approach, it does not evoke familiar images or a commonplace sense of school teaching. Established notions of "teaching," "learning," "research" and "clinical interview" already exist. However, established views often ignore human inquiry that is fundamentally multidimensional and evolving. In contrast, Critical Exploration focuses on furthering the multiple interpretations, by one or more learners, of the phenomenon they are encountering and acting on. The teacher's function is not to help the learner find a single correct meaning, but rather to find many, and to foster creative and collaborative efforts in learning.

The mind thrives in making connections among the ensemble of symbols that it develops over time; any single analogy, metaphor, or symbol, is almost always part of a larger family of such thought forms (Gruber, 1988; Gruber & Wallace, 2001)...In other words, any single idea is part of the individual's other thoughts about a given issue; and probably part of extended thoughts and feelings of others as they develop. Thus, the ensemble of multiple symbols and metaphors can be infinitely complex. Human learning thrives on this complexity and multiplicity. Duckworth (1996, 2001) and her colleagues demonstrate how this approach can effect learning—by studying the diverse symbolic meanings that people of different ages and occupations develop on different subjects at various places.

Critical Exploration thrives on tapping the ensemble of symbols that students develop in the classroom. This approach encourages and inspires students' creative thinking about the subject matter they study. Looking back from the present to the past of the development of this approach in education, we recognize the continual transformation of the Piagetian tradition. In his own view of education, Piaget was probably more insistent on promoting human potentials than being realistic about established schooling when he argued: "But for me, education means making creators, even if there aren't many of them, even if the creations of one are limited by comparison with those of another. But you have to make inventors, innovators, not conformists" (Bringuier, 1980, p. 132).

The making of creative people needs to be fueled by the creative spirit of the educator who seeks an inventor and an innovator in everyone, even in their own small way. One of the foremost scholars of creative thinking, Howard Gruber (2001) recommends Critical Exploration to "teachers and others who want to come to grips with fundamental problems facing all undefeated educators: What is thinking? How does it grow? How can learners, including the teachers, help each other?" By focusing on these fundamental issues in learning, this approach motivates educators to become inventors and innovators as well.

Critical Exploration is grounded in the process of teaching and learning, and practiced to inform teaching and learning. As Duckworth defined it in the beginning of this chapter, the approach deals directly with two major issues in school: curriculum and pedagogy. But it adds to them an emphasis on the development of human learning. So the two essential aspects of Critical Exploration in the classroom are *developing* curriculum and *developing* pedagogy. For those who have experienced the approach either as teacher, or student, or both, it is a promising approach not only for school, but for life.

REFERENCES

Ariasian, P.W., & Walsh, M.E. (1997). Constructivist cautions. *Phi Delta Kappan*, February, 444–449.

Bang, V. (1988). *Textes choisis* (Chosen texts). Genève, CH: Université de Genève.

Becker, C.S. (1986). Interviewing in human science research. *Methods*, 1, 101–124.

Bringuier, J. (1980). *Conversations with Jean Piaget*. Midway Reprint, Chicago: University of Chicago Press.

Claparède, E. (1925). The psychology of the child at Geneva and the J.J. Rousseau Institute. *Pedagogical Seminary*, 32, 92–104.

Delaney, M.K. (2001). Understanding the presidency. In E.R. Duckworth (Ed.), *Tell me more: Listening to learners explain*, pp. 125–144. New York: Teachers College Press.

Dixon, Jr., W.E. (2002). 20 studies that revolutionized child psychology. *Developments: Newsletter of the Society for Research in Child Development*, 45, (2), 1, 4.

Duckworth, E.R. (2003). L'Exploration critique dans la salle de classe (Critical Exploration in the classroom). Proceedings, Symposium in honor of Michael Huberman, October 19, 2002. Geneva, Switzerland.

Duckworth, E.R. (Ed.). (2001). *Tell me more: Listening to learners explain*. New York: Teachers College Press.

Duckworth, E.R. (1997). *Teacher to teacher: Learning from each other*. New York: Teachers College Press.

Duckworth, E.R. (1996). *The having of wonderful ideas*, 2nd ed. New York: Teachers College Press.

Duckworth, E.R. (1990). Opening the world. In E. R. Duckworth, J.Easley, D.Hawkins, & A. Henriques (Eds.), *Science education: A minds-on approach for the elementary years*. Hillsdale, NJ: Lawrence Erlbaum Associates.

Duckworth, E.R. (1987). Some depths and perplexities of elementary arithmetic. *Journal of Mathematical Behavior*, 6, 43–94.

Duckworth, E.R. (1986). *Inventing density*. Grand Forks, ND: North Dakota Study Group on Evaluation.

Duckworth, E.R., Julyan, C., & Rowe, T. (1985). Understanding equilibrium: The study of complex systems, final project report. Cambridge, MA: Educational Technology Center, Harvard Graduate School of Education.

Evans, R. (1973). *Jean Piaget: The man and his ideas*. New York: E.P.Dutton.

Frost, R. (1969). Design. In E.Lathem (Ed.), *The poetry of Robert Frost*. New York: Holt, Rinehart & Winston.

Gallagher, J., & Reid, D.K. (1981). *The learning theory of Piaget & Inhelder*. Monterey, CA: Brooks/Cole.

Ginsburg, H., & Opper, S. (1979). *Piaget's theory of intellectual development*, 2nd ed. Englewood Cliffs: Prentice-Hall.

Giorgi, A. (1985). The phenomenological psychology of learning and the verbal learning Tradition. In A.Giorgi (Ed.), *Phenomenology and psychological research*, pp. 23–85. Pittsburgh: Duquesne University Press.

Gruber, H.E. (2001). Book review comment. In E.R. Duckworth (Ed.), *Tell me more: Listening to learners explain*. New York: Teachers College Press.

Gruber, H.E. (1988). Coping with multiplicity and ambiguity of meaning in works of art. *Metaphor and Symbolic Activity*, 3, (3) 183–189.

Gruber, H.E., & Wallace, D.B. (2001). Creative work: The case of Charles Darwin. *American Psychologist*, 56, (4), 346–349.

Gruber, H.E., & Wallace, D.B. (1999). The case study method and evolving systems approach for understanding unique creative people at work. In R. Sternberg (Ed.), *Handbook of creativity*. New York: Cambridge University Press.

Gruber, H.E., & Vonèche, J.J. (Eds.) (1995). *The essential Piaget: An interpretive reference and guide* 2nd ed. Northvale, NJ: Jason Aronson.

Hawkins, D. (1994). Introduction. *The content of science: A constructivist approach to its teaching and learning*. London: The Falmer Press.

Hawkins, D. (1967). *Informed vision*. Boulder, CO: University of Colorado Press.

Hsueh, Y. (1998). Some notes about Bärbel Inhelder's 1954 study tour in the United States. *Archives de Psychologie*, 66, 239–254.

Hsueh, Y. (1994). From Piaget to pedagogy: Transformations in the constructivist teaching movement since 1973. Unpublished qualifying paper, Harvard Graduate School of Education, Cambridge, MA.

Inhelder, B. (1989). Bärbel Inhelder. In G. Lindsey (Ed.), *History of psychology in autobiography*, Vol. VIII, 209–244. Worcester, MA: Clark University Press.

Inhelder, B., Sinclair, H., & Bovet, M. (1974). *Learning and the development of cognition*. Cambridge, MA: Harvard University Press.

140   YEH HSUEH

Julyan, C., & Duckworth, E.R. (1996). A constructivist perspective on teaching and learning and learning science. In C.T. Fosnot (Ed.), *Constructivism: Theory, perspectives, and practice.* New York: Teachers College Press.

Mayer, S.J. (2003). The character of and academic response to Jean Piaget's clinical method in its early years. Unpublished qualifying paper, Harvard University Graduate School of Education. Cambridge, MA.

Nager, N., & Shapiro, E.K. (Eds.). (2000). *Revisiting a progressive pedagogy: The developmental interaction approach.* Albany, NY: State University of New York Press.

Osborne, J.W. (1990). Some basic existential-phenomenological research methodology for counselors. *Canadian Journal of Counseling, 24,* 79–91.

Piaget, J. (1995). Individuality in history: The individual and the education of reason. *J. Piaget: Sociological studies.* London: Routledge. (Originally published in 1933.)

Piaget, J. (1976). *To understand is to invent.* New York: Penguin Books. (Originally published in 1972.)

Piaget, J. (1966). *Judgment and reasoning in the child.* Totowa, NJ: Littlefield, Adams. (Originally published in 1924.)

Piaget, J. (1965). *The moral judgment of the child.* New York: The Free Press. (Originally published in 1932.)

Piaget, J. (1955). *The language and thought of the child.* New York: Meridian Books. (Originally published in 1923.)

Piaget, J. (1952b). *The origins of intelligence in children.* New York: International Universities Press.

Piaget, J. (1952a). Jean Piaget. In E.G. Boring, H. Werner, H.S. Langfeld & R.N. Yerkes(Eds.), *History of psychology in autobiography,* Vol. IV. Worcester, MA: Clark University Press. (Originally published in 1936.)

Piaget, J. (1933). Child psychology and the teaching of history. *The Quarterly Bulletin of the International Conference for the Teaching of History, 2,* 16–18.

Piaget, J. (1930). *The child's conception of physical causality.* London: Kegan Paul. (Originally published in 1927.)

Piaget, J. (1929). *The child's conception of the world.* New Jersey: Rowman & Littlefield. (Originally published in 1926.)

Piaget, J., & Garcia, R. (1989). *Psychogenesis and the history of science.* New York: Columbia University Press.

Polkinghorne, D.E. (1994). Research methodology in humanistic psychology. In F.Wertz (Ed.), *The humanistic movement: Recovering the person in psychology,* (pp. 105–128). Lake Forth, FL: Gardner.

Polkinghorne, D.E. (1989). Phenomenological research methods. In R.S. Valle & S.Halling (Eds.), *Existential-phenomenological perspectives in psychology,* (pp. 41–60). New York: Plenum.

Quintero, I.M. (2001). Children map their neighborhoods. In E.R. Duckworth (Ed.), *Tell me more: Listening to learners explain* (pp. 93–124). New York: Teachers College Press.

Reid, D.K., Kurkjian, C., & Carruthers, S.S. (1994). Special education teachers interpret constructivist teaching. *Remedial and Special Education, 15,* (5) 267–280)

Schneier, L.B. (2001). Apprehending poetry. In E.R. Duckworth (Ed.), *Tell me more: Listening to learners explain* (pp. 42–78). New York: Teachers College Press.

Schneier, L.B. (1990). "Why not just say it?"—Three case studies of understanding poetry. Unpublished qualifying paper at Harvard Graduate School of Education Cambridge, MA.

Tanner, J.M., & Inhelder, B. (1956). *Discussions on child development: A consideration of the biological, psychological, and cultural approaches to the understanding of human development and behaviour* (Geneva 1953–1956), Vols. 1–4. New York: International Universities Press.

Tobin, K., Tippins, D., & Gallard, A. (1993). Research on instructional strategies for teaching science. In D.L. Gabel (Ed.), *Handbook of research on science teaching and learning.* New York: MacMillan.

Von Glasersfeld, E. (1995). *Radical constructivism: A way of knowing and learning.* London: The Falmer Press.

8

MORAL RESPONSIBILITY AND CITIZENSHIP EDUCATION

Helen Haste

INTRODUCTION

Education for moral responsibility and for citizenship has been transformed in the last decade by global political changes and by the forefronting of concerns about moral responsibility, especially in relation to the environment. The question of how to educate for effective citizenship depends on recognizing the assumptions behind the goals of such education, and acknowledging the processes of development. What does the "competent citizen" look like? What factors in education and development facilitate such competence? There are longstanding tensions between the goals of conventional and unconventional political participation, and between educational agendas that regard knowledge or praxis, as the primary tools. These issues are discussed with illustrations from recent international studies relating to moral responsibility and citizenship education.

In the summer of 1983, I walked with Howard Gruber in the meadows of Oxford University while we were both attending the annual conference of the International Society for Political Psychology. He raised the question of "extraordinary moral responsibility"—the performance of actions or a consistent commitment to a pattern of moral behavior that went beyond the expected, challenged the dominant perspective, involving the actor in personal risk. Howard's concern with moral responsibility and moral creativity was longstanding and was part of his wider interest in creativity.

He argued that psychologists had an obligation to conduct rigorous and research in the field of moral responsibility and creativity. At that time, moral psychology was dominated by the pioneering work of Lawrence Kohlberg, whose theoretical model was grounded in empirical, longitudinal studies over more than twenty years and was well-founded in philosophical perspectives, especially the work of Baldwin, Dewey, Mead and Rawls. Kohlberg's research focused on moral reasoning, and particularly on the core moral concept of justice, and he identified six stages of development of increasing cognitive complexity in the understanding of justice (Colby & Kohlberg, 1987).

Could the Kohlberg theoretical framework encompass "extraordinary moral responsibility"? The data showed a strong relationship between certain kinds of activism and moral stage; in essence, the higher the moral stage, the more likely was an individual to feel personal responsibility to act in relation to their moral position and, also, the higher the moral stage, the more people saw public and societal issues as moral issues (Kohlberg & Candee 1984; Haste, 1986).

However, as Howard pointed out on that walk, very high stage moral reasoning is rare, and many individuals who are able to take extraordinary moral responsibility probably would not demonstrate high stage reasoning on the Kohlberg measure. Furthermore, the cognitive developmental approach focuses very much on the study of reasoning, ignoring both affect and "will."

Howard Gruber's own model for creativity in the wider context has taken what he terms the "evolving systems approach" (Gruber, 1981, 1986, 1989). Exceptionally gifted people (he studied Darwin and Piaget in great depth) have a wide and interconnected "network of enterprise," they have a sense of purpose and will that gives direction to their lives on a daily and a longer term basis, and this permeates their whole network. They tend to utilize "images of wide scope," often powerful metaphors that play a key role in their innovative thinking. They also maintain a powerful affective tie to the problems, or phenomena, that are being investigated. In studying such people, Gruber monitored all aspects of the developmental process: the organisation of knowledge, the purpose pursued by the individual, and the affective experiences involved.

This is a "whole system" model; a full understanding of creativity requires the larger picture, and the relationship between the individual and key others, including also the cultural and social context. It is an approach that requires a long time scale, and intensive individual case studies. It lends itself to an in-depth understanding of particular individuals, including the "exceptional" person.

Gruber hoped that psychologists might find ways to explore moral creativity which took a larger view, one that might encompass these dimensions, and also inform citizenship education. He himself did not conduct research in this area, but he was instrumental in facilitating some studies, and much discussion (Haste, 1989, 1990). In the falls of 1983 and 1985, at Gruber's instigation, the Social Science Research Council committee on Learning, Development and Giftedness[i] hosted conferences at Yale and in New York City on concepts and methodologies relating to moral creativity. One project that was stimulated by this was the study of extraordinary individuals, "moral exemplars," by Anne Colby and William Damon (Colby & Damon 1992). Twenty-three individuals nominated for their exceptional moral responsibility were interviewed in depth to find out what motivated them. This study, interestingly, underscored the point about moral reasoning stages; there was little relationship between moral stage and moral commitment.

More recently, Gardner, Damon and Csikszentmihalyi (2001) have produced an extended study of moral responsibility among professionals and leaders, which explores the conflicts between market pressures and ethical concerns.

In 1983 the world was divided into East and West, with an ever-present threat of nuclear accident. The extraordinary moral responsibility that preoccupied Gruber and others at that time concerned peace activism in particular, which was conceptualised as part of a citizen's larger responsibility to act as watchdog and whistleblower. The key question for psychology was what motivated a person first to become engaged morally with a "public" issue, and second, to feel able to take action.

Major changes since 1983 have quite transformed the framework within which both the study of extraordinary moral responsibility, and the creation of a blueprint for citizenship education, can be formulated. The changes have been in the global political world, with significant knock-on effects for national identity, definitions of democracy, and for education agendas. There have been changes in the domains that are associated with activism. There have been changes within the theoretical frameworks of psychology itself.

CITIZENSHIP AND MORAL RESPONSIBILITY

The main agenda for this paper is to consider the present state of debate around citizenship education, and to relate this to the concept of moral responsibility.

The domains of both moral responsibility and citizenship sensitize us to an important feature of psychological work; it cannot be divorced from real-world events. In fact, psychologists have been remarkably un-prescient about predicting major social movements. We neither predicted ethnic identity movements nor the rise of gender consciousness; nor did we (or anyone else) predict the dissolution of the Cold War and the East-West divide. However, psychologists have monitored these social changes, and some key assumptions inherent in psychology have been modified through this work.

The decade of the nineteen nineties was a natural laboratory for po-litical, social and psychological change. First, the global political situation was totally transformed with far-reaching implications and dramatic ef-fects. Second, there have been major shifts in the dominant social values that impinge on citizenship and moral responsibility—most notably the rise of environmentalism (Harré, Muhlhausler & Brockmeier, 1999; Kahn, 1999). Thirdly, significant public debates have forefronted ethical concerns particularly in relation to scientific and technological developments; these have made public accountability more salient.

I shall explore how these global changes have so profoundly affected the definitions of "citizenship"' and "citizenship education," in both East and West. I shall also explore how moral responsibility has become salient as a consequence of shifts in dominant social values. I will also look at three rather different studies relating to citizenship issues.

The first study by Torney-Purta, Lehmann, Oswald and Schulz (2001) explored citizenship and education in 28 nations and involved 90,000 14-year olds, and 8000 teachers. Eleven nations were Western European, 11 were former Eastern bloc; the remaining six were the US, Chile, Colombia, Cyprus, Hong Kong and Australia. This study covered a number of issues relevant to the current discussion, including politi-cal knowledge, current and expected participation, and teachers' expec-tations and values in relation to what should be taught in citizenship education.

The second study, by Van Hoorn, Komlosi. Suchar and Samelson (1999), provides data on cultural processes in practice, and how these cul-tural contexts work at the level of the individual. It is longitudinal data, covering the period from 1991 to 1995, a period of major transition. The authors interviewed a total of 153 17-year olds in 1991–2 in three cities: Pecs and Budapest in Hungary, and Gdansk in Poland.

The third study, conducted by Haste and Tyrrell (2002), involved adolescents in four British schools. The focus was on personal effi-cacy, both through self-rating scales and participants' intentions regard-ing community-related actions. We also investigated values relating to environmental issues. The results showed marked differences between schools and genders.

CITIZENSHIP EDUCATION

The issues in citizenship education are how to conceptualize the "good" and "effective" citizen and how to generate educational programs to produce such citizens. In relatively stable nation states, these agendas are mainly responsive to what are perceived to be the requirements of the status quo. In times of change and reconstruction, the task of defining "the citizen", and generating educational programs, is proactive rather than reactive: to ensure that the growing individual is properly prepared for a new role in a new world.

There are two over-riding issues about the assumptions that we make in developing a program of citizenship education:

- what kind of "citizen" are we trying to produce, equipped for what kind of democracy?
- what processes do we think will be effective in producing such citizens?

These issues entail three questions;

- what should be our goals?
- how should we go about citizenship education?
- what should be the content of the curriculum?

Certain central tensions underpin these questions. There is a long-recognized underlying tension surrounding the desirable goals of citizenship education. This tension is between "conventional" goals—encouraging participation in the existing system—and the goal of challenging the system. There is also a tension regarding the way in which citizenship education should be conducted; should the emphasis be on knowledge of the country's history and traditions, and the constitution—or should the emphasis be on praxis? Praxis means providing the student with forms of experience that are presumed to translate into appropriate skills, either through simulated activities in the classroom, or the opportunity for real-life experiences in citizenship. The actual components of citizenship are under contention; should the emphasis be on values education, on knowledge about social institutions, on critical thinking, or on participation?

Goals

Inculcating appropriate skills for inhabiting the status quo reflects T.H. Marshall's widely accepted definition of citizenship distinguishing the civic, the political and the social. These are different areas of rights and obligations, and also of understanding and knowledge (Marshall, 1977). This definition has influenced research on the development of citizens, and it influences curriculum development.

Marshall's model of citizenship chimed with research on conventional forms of political activity, such as voting and participating in institutional forms of lobbying. With the upheavals of the period 1967–1987—student protest, Vietnam, and the Peace Movement—research shifted to the psychological parameters of unconventional and confrontational political activity (Kaase, 1990). A clear profile of the citizen as activist emerged—a person with a strong sense of efficacy and agency and low trust in government (Marsh, 1977; Haste, 1993).

After the era of protest and the end of the Cold War, research emphasis shifted to competence—what makes some young people engage in community activity, take responsibility and leadership? This was not a return to looking at conventional participation in existing institutions; it reflected a view of the citizen working for improvement and change. The "competent" young looked not unlike the protesters (Hart & Fegley, 1995; Lenhart & Rabiner, 1995; Yates & Youniss, 1999).

In the last decade in the West, however, there has been growing concern about young people's political apathy. The impetus for research and development in citizenship or civic education springs in part from this (Ichilov, 1998). In Britain, a recent blueprint for citizenship education spells out the necessity for an active citizenry who can challenge as well as participate (Crick, 1998). This document echoes many of the lessons from research on the cultural antecedents of young people's engagement, such as active involvement in school governance and in initiatives in the community (Hahn, 1998; Flanagan et al., 1998).

CHANGING DEFINITIONS AND VALUES

In 1992, the philosopher Francis Fukuyama declared an "end to history" on the grounds that "liberal democracy" reflected the highest state that society could reach (Fukuyama, 1992). While his optimism was widely questioned, it reflected the euphoria that followed the breakdown of the former communist bloc.

The end of the communist era presented challenges to those researching concepts of democracy and political understanding, as well as to those who had the very real practical task of creating a new democracy. It had an impact on the West as well as the East. The hard economic and political realities of the nineties confronted definitions and practices that formerly were either taken for granted, or regarded with uncritical optimism. For example, Western psychologists—particularly in the US—treated the concept of "democracy" in the terms used in the United States, with concomitant implications for educational practice. It soon became clear that some definitions and assumptions that prevailed in the USA were not necessarily transportable to the Eastern-bloc nations.

Most obviously, in former Soviet bloc communities, the task was to re-invent not only democracy but national identity. The common task was to eradicate communist ideology; the problem was to find an adequately comprehensive replacement on which to base civic education. In so doing, each former Eastern bloc country has sought its own cultural framework, defined explicitly by reclaiming its national history, within which to develop both new conceptions of democracy and new conceptions of national identity (Torney-Purta, Schwille & Amadeo, 1999). Under USSR rule, national identity was supposedly subsumed by a larger identification with the communist world; covert national identity therefore fuelled resistance. Several countries report a dual consciousness during the Soviet era, where all citizens were aware of two quite different versions of history and culture—the official and the unofficial. (Wertsch, 1998; Valdmaa, 1999). So the reconstruction of national identity became merged with the construction of a nationally appropriate form of democracy.

Changes in global politics have also modified a primary form of activist politics—the peace movement. Peace movements still exist, directed at specific areas of conflict, such as the former Yugoslavia, and the Israeli-Palestinian conflict. They have been re-activated also by September 11. But the niche of global concern that was occupied by peace activism directed against nuclear warfare has arguably been replaced by other global issues, in particular environmental and ecology movements.

The rise of environmentalism has provided us with new questions relating to moral responsibility and citizenship. It reflects a quite major change in dominant social values. Environmentalism has some striking attributes. First, it is not tied explicitly to a left- or right-wing ideology. There are left and right versions of environmentalism, based on differing ideological assumptions, that correlate with other measures of the left-right spectrum. However, the moral dimensions of environmentalism spring from a different source than traditional political allegiances (Harré, Muhlhausler & Brockmeier, 1999).

Second, environmental concerns engage categories of people who have not traditionally been politically efficacious. Notably, concern about the environment captures the imagination and commitment even of young children (Kahn, 1999). Furthermore, it is associated with action, both personal action in relation to domestic practices such as waste disposal and the selection of consumer items, and public or political action such as campaigning. Environmental concern has very rapidly become a central issue, as can be seen in its role in mainstream school curricula worldwide. For example, it was designated a major strand of social and moral education in a British blueprint for social and moral education, alongside more traditional value domains like Society, The Self, and Relationships (SCAA, 1996). In the IEA study (The International Association for the Evaluation of Educational Achievement), over 90% of teachers considered that learning about protecting the environment was important (Torney-Purta, Lehmann, Oswald & Schulz, 2001).

Environmentalism is part of a major value shift–toward ethical issues–that has occurred in the last couple of decades. In response to public pressure, there has been a remarkable change in the accountability of business enterprises. Both legislation and rhetoric have combined to make businesses explicit about their practices in relation to the use of resources and the management of waste. This has affected more than practice; it has resulted in making ethical awareness itself a public requirement. One example of this is the increasing popularity of "ethical investment," which has acted as a pressure on companies, as well as threats of consumer action withdrawing custom from non-green organisations (Lewis, 2002). This is more than a debate about the environment; it has made ethical discussion itself salient in areas where it was not formerly found.

Public debate about ethics has also become salient for science and technology. The longstanding argument from the scientific community that the pursuit of scientific knowledge is value-free and that it can be separated from any consequences of its applications, has been challenged. This is in part a spin-off from movements to improve public understanding of science which, in turn, reveal widespread lay concern about the ethical dimensions of scientific advances, concern that is central to negative attitudes toward science. The efforts to find rapprochement between expert and lay communities, culminating in Britain in the recent House of Lords report on Science and Society (2000), have made at least the British scientific community aware of the need to enter the public debate and show that ethical concerns are being respected.

These developments were in part fuelled by environmentalist rhetoric and concerns; in part however they tapped into longstanding cultural anxieties about both the ethics and the possible risks of "interfering with nature." Both cloning and genetically modified (GM) foods have created a furore (especially in Britain), reflected in intense media discussion. A practical outcome has been detailed labelling of food products and disclaimers by many food suppliers about GM ingredients. The rhetorical effect has been to legitimize the public ethical scrutiny of activities that "meddle with Nature."

These various strands have contributed to the increasing centrality of ethics. The discussion of ethics is in the public domain and is deemed a legitimate, even mandatory, activity for all concerned persons. Such activity has become a normal field for research, and demands for public engagement on ethical issues are reflected in the development of curricula in moral and citizenship education. Taking ethical responsibility, and making preparations for citizenship that overtly reflect ethics, are on the agenda in ways that they were not in 1983.

COMPETENCE

Let us consider first the concept of competence. What do we mean by competence in relation to citizenship and moral responsibility? Competence is more than a domain-based skill. It implies effective interaction and agency in the physical, social and cultural world. It must involve self-regulation, monitoring and initiative-taking. It must incorporate adaptation. It implies effectiveness not only in performance, but in the interpretation of context and meaning. Competence includes knowing what one needs and does not need to know. Such understanding comes from recognizing the context in which one's skills function in effective interaction with the environment.

Competence has been quite extensively studied. The "competent" individual is self-sufficient, able to focus attention and plan, has a future orientation, is adaptable to change, has a sense of responsibility, has a belief that one can have an effect, and is capable of commitment. These characteristics are fostered by families that provide competent role models, give encouragement and affirmation, set goals, and assign responsibilities that are seen to contribute to the household; and by cohesive communities that give the individual responsibilities, and the chance to acquire skills that contribute to the public good. In sum, to feel agentic requires the experience of being able to have an effect on one's environment, either alone or more usually with others (Call, Mortimer & Shanahan, 1995; Colby & Damon, 1992; Fogelman, 1994; Hamilton & Fenzel, 1988; Hart & Fegley, 1995; Lenhart & Rabiner, 1995; Morris, 1992; Paolicchi, 1995).

Other studies show that adult political and community participation springs not from adolescent political party involvement but from youthful community involvement—particularly for girls (Youniss, McLellan & Yates, 1997: Hart, Atkins & Ford, 1998; Roker, Player & Coleman 1999).

I have elsewhere explored for a range of competences that I regard as essential in the immediate future—although cultural context would determine exactly how they are manifested (Haste 2001). The ones relevant to citizenship education are agency and responsibility, finding and sustaining community links, and dealing with ambiguity and diversity. Within the description of each competence, I demonstrate some inherent tensions, and the implications for education.

Agency and Responsibility

To take responsibility means to recognise that one is an agent, and that one can act upon one's inclinations. However, "responsibility" is a complex term that needs unpacking. I have explored three different meanings of this term that reflect conflicting ideas of both the processes and goals of moral and citizenship education. They also reflect the tensions between conventional and unconventional forms of activity (Kaase, 1990; Haste, 1993).

Responsibility 1 I define as duties and obligations to the community; the agenda of expectations, rules and mores set by the community. Here, the educational task is to make young people aware of these obligations and duties and to foster the values and motivations that will lead to their assuming these responsibilities voluntarily.

A moral tension implicit in Responsibility 1 is the classic question of whether morality is the performance of proactive, prosocial action, or the avoidance of antisocial action. Proactive morality may, on occasion, require the individual to resist normative pressures—whether the pressures of accepted codes, or the specific social pressures of the group. A moral system that valorises duty and obligation, and therefore conformity to norms, is open to the question of whether this would inhibit the individual agent from, for example, whistle-blowing.

Responsibility 2 I define as the sense of connection to others that generates caring and concern. It is the corollary of a perspective that emphasizes relationships and interpersonal ties. In recent psychological discourse on moral development, this has tended to be defined mainly in terms of Gilligan's critique of Kohlberg's theory of moral development, specifically that Kohlberg's ethical system privileges reasoning about justice, ignoring the ethic of care and responsibility. Gilligan argued that women are more likely to use an ethic of care, and men, an ethic of justice (Gilligan, 1982). Behind Gilligan's (and others') perspective on care and connection is recognition that the individual is embedded in a social context, in interconnection with others (Noddings, 1984; Hekman, 1995). Justice reasoning, in contrast, starts from an assumption of individual autonomy, and the need therefore to balance the respective rights, interests and obligations of all those involved in the situation, to arrive at the most "just" solution. So, in the justice-based model, individuals are conceived of as separate, not as connected.

Responsibility 2 should not be conceptualized only as a contrast to an ethical system based on reasoning about justice. If people are inevitably interconnected, competence involves effective negotiation of interaction, dialogue and the social processes involved in creating meaning and shared consensus—the competence to connect with others, towards ends that serve the mutual needs of the group, network or community.

Responsibility 3 I define as a sense of personal commitment to carry through one's value position into action and engagement. It carries with it the implication of personal efficacy and competence, and also motivation. Responsibility 3 is often couched in the individualistic terminology of autonomy: "I have arrived at my personal moral position and the logical imperative is that I act upon this." However, Responsibility 3 can also be seen as arising from discursive and linguistic practices and, therefore, through interaction with others. In particular, one is positioned as a reflective actor in a "moral" drama, one that requires certain kinds of action for which one is uniquely responsible. Responsibility 3 is perhaps the closest to Gruber's concept of "extraordinary moral responsibility" (Haste, 1990, 1993).

Finding and Sustaining Community Links

In this competence, we see issues that apply to the processes of development and their implication for the practices of education. Research has demonstrated the importance of school climate, elusive though this concept is. The classic British work by Rutter, Maugham, Mortimore, and Ouston in 1979, *fifteen thousand hours*, a meticulous longitudinal study of twelve secondary schools in London, showed that key characteristics of schools as social institutions had a significant effect on academic performance and good behavior. These characteristics included teacher actions in lessons, expectations of students, conditions for students, incentives and rewards, and the extent to which children were able to take responsibility.

Contemporary with Rutter et al.'s study in Britain, in the United States Lawrence Kohlberg was experimenting with the "just community" in schools (Power, Higgins & Kohlberg, 1989; Higgins, 1991). This derived from Dewey's principles of democratic education and the importance of hands-on experience of sharing in decision-making. The original purpose of the just community was to create an environment in which reasoning about moral and social issues was transparent, and in which dialogue stimulated the development of moral reasoning. But just as interesting as the effect on individual reasoning, was the moral atmosphere or norms that developed in the group. This work originally stemmed from a focus on individual cognition; however, it can be interpreted in terms of the social constructionist perspective that looks at how dialogic processes create a community ethos (Edwards & Mercer, 1987; Bruner, 1996).

More recent studies of political development show that open discussion in the classroom, and a feeling that one is part of a school community, foster civic commitment and engagement (Hahn, 1998; Flanagan et al., 1998).

What is being fostered here is the competence to be part of a collective community, taking responsibility for that participation and the tasks shared by the community. Children become skilled in understanding not only what is expected of them, but how to be engaged and active in the process of production. The school climate facilitates—or otherwise—competencies in judgement, taking and sharing responsibility, and in leadership. These are transferable to other community settings; the more children can practice both the skills and the understanding, the more able they will be to utilise them in a larger setting.

Behind this approach are certain assumptions about how the school functions as a community. Firstly, people are social beings who generate meaning through discourse and social interaction, and through cultural repertoires, stories and scripts transmitted by social practices and narratives. The desirable goals are values that will promote engagement with the community, and foster an individual sense of meaning, and a stable community. It follows that procedures to attain the goals must harness these social and psychological processes. These include:

~ values being enacted as social practice, a taken-for-granted-part of everyday life;

~ social identity being fostered through stories and narratives about the community and culture .

~ through experiencing responsibility and caring, as giver and receiver, the individual can feel engaged with, and connected to, others.

~ helping community members to recognise that institutions and communities have multiple agendas, and to understand community processes and foster pluralist values.

~ through awareness of the community's norms, and reflection upon them, social processes become explicit, and it becomes possible consciously to generate new values and behaviors. (Haste, 1996)

Dealing with Ambiguity and Diversity

Managing multiculturalism and pluralism can be seen from two different perspectives. One is a value perspective: that we should cultivate the virtues of tolerance, justice and consideration for others. This reflects goals of education. However, my concern here is with the other, epistemological perspective: how we know, and how we can know. This reflects processes of education.

There has been a strong intellectual and cultural tradition, in the West at least, which privileges problem solving, and so generates anxieties about ambiguity and uncertainty, which become strong and culturally-endorsed motives for finding the single "right answer." In fact, research has thrown into question the assumption that ambiguity is disequilibrating, anxiety inducing and will produce motives to reduce uncertainty. In practice, we are able to juggle a number of disparate and dissonant values or beliefs, and to move between different and contrasting discourses. Naturalistic research, which looks at narrative and discourse in contrast to the artificial constraints of enforced experimental designs, shows that we are very adept at dealing with ambiguity and multiple perspectives.

One striking example is Michael Billig's study of British people talking, in family conversations, about the Royal Family (Billig, 1992). There are several value perspectives on the Royal family, which are inherently contradictory, e.g., that they are expensive, an outdated luxury that drains the country's resources, that they serve a useful symbolic function, and perform important public services. Billig's work showed that people move smoothly and without anxiety from one apparently contradictory statement to another. He concluded that we operate with several parallel discourses, each of which is subjectively internally consistent. It is evident that we are very skilled in picking up the cues about which discourse is in place, and fitting in with it.

Education for dealing with ambiguity, therefore, is more than preaching the virtues of pluralism and multiculturalism; it involves teaching how to manage multiple discourses effectively and creatively. It is both a value issue and a cognitive issue.

A STUDY OF COMPETENCE

In a British study with 290 15-year olds, Claire Tyrrell and I investigated beliefs about efficacy, about obedience to the law, and about helping the community, and values relating to the environment. This study involved four single–sex schools, two private and two in the state system.

The seven factors that emerged from a factor analysis revealed not only constellations of similar beliefs, but also a conjunction of certain values with beliefs about personal efficacy. There were gender differences on all factors, and also school differences reflecting social class.

The first factor was concern about the environment, which reflected an active preoccupation with environmental and welfare concerns, and a sense of personal efficacy. Girls scored higher than boys on this factor. The second factor was community responsibility and efficacy, and drew out active reflection on social issues and a proactive desire to become involved. Girls scored higher on this factor, and there was also a significant contrast between the girls' private school and the boys' public school. On the third factor, primarily about areas of personal efficacy such as social and manual skills, boys scored higher than girls, but private school boys scored higher than public school boys.

Boys, especially the public school boys, were considerably more alienated than girls. The public school boys stood out as being least likely to agree that people should "obey the law" or that they "would make personal sacrifices to help people in need." They were also the most likely to agree that "I don't think that anything I do will have any effect on social and environmental problems." While this study did reveal a generally high level of concern about the environment and about helping the community, the gender differences and school differences raise questions both about social class and school culture, which further study needs to explore. However the most interesting finding is the conjunction between social values around concern for the environment and welfare, and sense of efficacy.

TENSIONS

There are several key issues to address in citizenship education, all of which have implications for moral responsibility. There are tensions around the concept of the "autonomous person" which reflect both the goals of education and assumptions about the processes of human development, and therefore, educational practice.

Psychology wavered throughout the 20th century between seeing humans as passive and moulded by external forces, and seeing them as active agents in relation to their experience. "Agency" implies that one actively interacts with one's environment, including active engagement with one's own learning and development. The implication of having agency is that the individual has a sense of efficacy and a sense of being able to take an initiative. It implies that the individual has a role in constructing meaning and interpretation, even if such constructions take place through negotiation with others, in a cultural context (Wertsch, 1998).

The discussion of agency, however, needs to be conducted with an appreciation of challenges to the Western ideal of autonomy, challenges that have far-reaching implications for educational practice as well as for core values. Western culture has tended to equate individual moral maturity with resisting collective pressure. In such a context, individualistic values and the psychological competence to think for oneself and resist social pressure are valued and fostered. Autonomy therefore is seen as the expression of moral and intellectual maturity (Haste, Helkama & Markoulis, 1998).

Recent critiques of these assumptions arise from a major shift in perspectives about how we actually become effective participants in our culture. Rather than this being the successful outcome of an individual developmental struggle in which, in effect, the self is a personal creation, there has been a shift to seeing such competence as arising from reflective appreciation and management of one's membership in the community, as I explored in relation to the competence "finding and sustaining community links" (Harré & Gillett, 1994; Harré, 1998).

Critics question the ontological assumptions behind a model of the autonomous human (Taylor, 1991; Bell, 1993; Shotter, 1993; Harré, 1998). Their position is that autonomy is based on an illusion that the human being functions in social isolation. Within this illusion we focus only on "inside the head" cognitive processes, seeing ourselves as engaging in an ethical monologue, and ignoring the social, cultural and linguistic dialogue through which all our competences are fostered. Taylor, for example, argues that human life is fundamentally dialogic. Shotter and Harré argue that the primary human reality is face-to-face conversation.

If social interaction is the crucible of meaning, then learning morality (or any other competence) happens through explicit and implicit discourse and social practices. The "meaning" of something—including the meaning of our own identity and morality—depends on what is comprehensible and recognised within our social community. We are members of multiple communities each of which offers us identity and personal meaning; and within each, different elements, skills and competences are salient.

THE ASSUMPTIONS BEHIND THE CURRICULUM

Methods of teaching, and philosophies of education, divide quite sharply between knowledge-based modes of what people should know and understand about citizenship and praxis-based models of how to give people the experiences through which they can become effective citizens, the opportunities for self-determination, and engagement with the processes of decision-making in the school and wider community. This division pervades discussions of civic education. How far is knowledge of institutions, procedures, and history sufficient or necessary for young people to become personally engaged in their community? How far is learning to be an efficacious citizen dependent on mediated experience of some kind of personal action?

Behind the agenda of knowledge-based education often lies the assumption of a "canon", a body of knowledge, a repository of the essential elements of culture that "every child should know." The concept of a canon reflects very precisely one aspect of the tension between continuity and innovation: Is the purpose of the canon to reproduce culture by equipping the young to carry on the traditions, or is it to provide the competence to face the challenges of novelty and innovation (Gardner, 1999)?

At a time of rapid change, there is a very explicit question about what should comprise a new canon to meet the requirements of a new world. In societies that are stable, however, we see a somewhat different tension, especially where multiculturalism becomes a major discourse. This raises the question of whether the canon perpetuates a particular cultural heritage. Some who espouse certain forms of multiculturalism wish to avoid the dominance of a unitary "White Western male" canon, and to replace it—or at least supplement it—with a canon that expresses the cultural values of minorities. Others are wary of what they see as the implied relativism of multiculturalism, and wish to bolster some consensual canon as the bastion against fragmentation and the loss of "high culture".

The recent British report on citizenship education (Crick, 1998) comes down firmly on praxis; its three prescriptions for "effective education for citizenship" are "learning self-confidence and social and morally responsible behavior both in and beyond the classroom," "learning about and becoming helpfully involved in the life and concerns of their community, including learning through community involvement and service to the community," and "learning about and how to make themselves effective in public life through knowledge, skills and values" (p. 12–13).

THE IEA STUDY

The IEA study (Torney-Purta et al., 2001) provides data from 28 nations on a number of issues highly salient to these discussions:

~ what knowledge do students possess.
~ what have students learned, according to their own perceptions.
~ what do teachers believe students should learn.
~ what teachers believe should be the priorities for how learning should take place, and how does this differ from what they perceive to be educational priorities.
~ what students are currently participating in, and what they expect to participate in, in the future.
~ the relationship between knowledge and behavior.

Knowledge

In looking at country comparisons of civic knowledge —measured by a range of items concerning the understanding of democratic principles and processes—some interesting patterns emerge. There was quite a wide range of performance. Civic knowledge was higher than average in several middle European, former Eastern bloc countries (Poland, the Czech Republic, the Slovak Republic), in Finland and Norway, in Greece, Italy and Cyprus, and in the US and Hong Kong. It was lower than average in the former soviet Baltic States, in Portugal and Belgium, and in Romania, Chile and Colombia. The other Western European countries, and Australia and Hungary also scored moderately on civic knowledge.

In terms of student perception of what they had learnt, it appears that, overall, over 80% learn to cooperate with others, and understand people with different ideas. Protecting the environment has become a world-wide concern with 79% of students saying they have learnt this. Some figures were lower; 72% report learning to be concerned about what happens in other countries, and only 68% had learned the importance of contributing to solving the problems of the community. Only 58% said they had learned the importance of voting.

Teachers' Perceptions

When teachers were asked what children should be taught, over 90% included national history and obeying the law. In only 3 countries (Denmark, Sweden and Switzerland) was protecting the environment deemed important by less than 90% of the sample and in only five countries (Denmark, England, Hong Kong, Norway and Switzerland) did less than 90% of the sample consider recognizing the importance of promoting human rights to be desirable. On the other hand, belonging to a political party was seen as important by more than 20% of teachers only in Cyprus (51%) and Romania (32%). On other, "unconventional" behaviors, over

60% overall considered that participating in peaceful protest was a desirable behavior, rising to over 80% for 11 countries. In all countries except Hungary and Hong Kong, over 55% considered that students should be aware of the importance of ignoring a law that violated human rights; in 8 countries this rose to 85%.

Teachers' views on what should constitute the curriculum, and the processes of education, reflect the tension between knowledge and praxis, and those regarding what are seen to be the best route to efficacy and engagement. What should schools be prioritizing? What are they prioritizing? Teachers were given four options; knowledge, participation, values, and critical thinking. The most common pattern—in 15 countries—was that knowledge was generally perceived to be the dominant agenda but that it should be the least important of the four. Only Portugal placed knowledge as the desired first priority. Participation was overwhelmingly seen as being the lowest actual priority for schools (in 20 countries), but the majority placed it third in desirability. Only Germany, Cyprus and Lithuania placed it as a first desirable priority. Critical thinking and values were rated as high priorities with nearly all countries placing these first or second. Critical thinking, however, was not perceived as an actual first school priority in any country. Values, in contrast, were seen generally as the schools' actual priority in five countries—Belgium, Bulgaria, Chile, England and Slovenia.

Action and Participation

Current participation was relatively infrequent, particularly for overtly political activity. Twenty-eight percent of students reported being members of a school council. The same proportion also reported collecting money for charities. Eighteen percent took part in voluntary activities and 15% belonged to environmental organisations. Only 6% were members of human rights organisations, and only 5% of political party youth groups.

The distinction made by Kaase (1990) between conventional and unconventional participation, and between legal and illegal unconventional participation, is useful for our purposes as it picks up the difference between the more conforming kinds of responsibility, and responsibility that requires independent action and moral engagement. Overall, the vast majority of young citizens expected, in the future, to vote—over 80% in 17 of the countries. In 11 countries, over 60% expected to collect money for social causes. Unconventional legal activities included collecting signatures for a petition and taking part in non-violent demonstrations. Here the figures were lower, but in 14 countries, over 45% expected to collect signatures and in 9 countries, over 45% would take part in a demonstration.

There were gender differences, with girls more likely to vote, collect money and signatures, and boys more likely to participate in a demonstration. Expected participation in illegal activities—spray-painting slogans, blocking traffic and occupying buildings—was expected more rarely (between 14% and 18% of the sample) and significantly more by boys than girls.

Relationship Between Knowledge and Action

The report shows that knowledge and intended voting behavior at the individual level are strongly related—level of civic knowledge predicts intention to vote. However, taking only the patterns across countries, and including all forms of participation, both conventional and unconventional, it appears from the tables that knowledge did not always predict participation. Three countries emerged as high in civic knowledge, high in students valuing participation, both conventional and unconventional, and in the expectation of adult participation. These were Cyprus, Poland and the United States. In contrast, five countries emerged as low in civic knowledge but high in expected adult participation—Chile, Colombia, Lithuania, Romania and Portugal. Two countries had a high level of knowledge but low participation both now and expected in adult life—these were the Czech Republic and Finland.

A substantial number of countries with medium level of civic knowledge had a low level of current participation and a low level of expected future participation. These were Australia, Denmark, England, Slovenia, Sweden and Switzerland. In some countries, there was an expected high level of participation in unconventional or social movement activity but low expected involvement with conventional activity—this included Norway and Russia.

A CASE STUDY OF CHANGE AND PARTICIPATION

The IEA study is very suggestive of the power of cultural factors and of the effects of history. It also suggests that teachers have quite a clear perception of what does, and does not work in creating "responsible" and active citizens.

The study by Van Hoorn, Komlosi, Suchar, and Samelson (1999) provides longitudinal data on cultural processes in practice, and how these cultural contexts work at the level of the individual. The interviews focused

on personal ambitions, sense of optimism about both the self and the socio-
political situation, and concepts such as democracy and freedom. The authors interviewed a total of 153 17-year olds in 1991–2, in three cities: Pecs
and Budapest in Hungary, and Gdansk in Poland. The Budapest sample
was an elite group, attending a school with exceptional access to English
and to foreign cultural influences through educational exchanges. The Pecs
and Gdansk samples attended regular schools. Follow-up interviews were
conducted in 1993–4 in both Pecs and Gdansk, and in 1993 and 1995 in
Budapest.

The study captures a unique moment. At the time of the first interviews in 1991 there was still a sense of excitement about the recent
dramatic changes—and an awareness of the problems they had brought,
especially economic. In the first interviews, all the young people, but
particularly the Budapest elite sample, demonstrated a high level of interest in the social and political situation, and were optimistic about
change. They saw opportunities for themselves in the new Hungary and
Poland.

By 1993, considerable disillusion had set in, both about the changing
political world and about opportunities. Economic problems were apparent, and though respondents discussed them primarily in terms of their
own family experiences, they alluded to the widening gap between rich and
poor. But also in Hungary, there had briefly been a nationalistic, rightwing
government that was quite anti-Semitic. By 1995, the Hungarian government was more socialist and the respondents were more satisfied, though
they were not more optimistic about the economic situation.

The Hungarian samples were more sophisticated than the Gdansk
sample. This surprised the authors, who expected that young people growing up in the crucible of Solidarity, many of whose family members had
been directly involved, would find political change more salient. The Polish
young people were in general less enthusiastic about democracy and individual freedom, and were more cynical. In 1992, 62% of Polish youngsters considered democracy the best system, but by 1994 only 24% thought
so (Cichowicz, 1993; CBOS 1994). This may reflect the extreme prolifera-
tion of political parties in Poland—120 at that time—and the disillusionment following both from this and from economic problems. However,
they were also conceptually less sophisticated; they defined freedom (especially in the first round) in terms of lack of personal constraints and a
simplistic free market economy—with perceived concomitant jungle warfare consequences.

The Hungarian young people were exposed to better citizenship education programs in school than were the Polish youngsters, with clear
effects on the development of concepts. In 1991, democracy meant a

multi-party system, freedom of speech and the ability to influence political leaders. By 1995, this was considerably elaborated to include free elections, free press and a representative government that served the needs of the people and ensured a good standard of living for all. On the matter of freedom, in 1991 the emphasis was on "being able to do what one wants"; by 1995, this was tempered by recognition of the need for legal constraints and responsibility.

The authors explored the relationship between personal development and socio-political context. At least for the Pecs and Gdansk samples, personal relationships with family and friends were by far the most salient elements in identity and identity development. They also focused on the effects of the political and economic changes for this immediate circle. The Budapest sample had a broader concept of community and a greater awareness of the outside world—probably due to their experience, as well as to the nature of their education. They were better able to see their own ambitions in the context of the larger changes—even though they, also, had become disillusioned and disengaged by 1995.

In these data, we can see the creation of new concepts of democracy, and the implied psychological processes that are being harnessed to ensure effective education. The roles of national identity and of folk memory turn out to be highly salient—and more complex than has been assumed in the West, where nationalism is associated with conservatism. It is clear from the Hungarian interviews particularly, that national identity, and its role in the construction of a new Hungarian democracy, was a part of the optimistic picture of these liberal young people—and that they were wary indeed when a government came into power that wanted to translate this into exclusivity and bounded ethnicity.

This study does reveal very clearly that young people formulate their conceptions of democracy and freedom not as a direct transmission of what they have been told—whether from the school or the media—but through a transformation via their personal experiences and those of their families. This is an uneven developmental process, and it is dialectical. This is very evident in the interviews. There is diversity in conceptual complexity, and there is a definite progression (particularly with the elite sample), but what is interesting is the interweaving of the students' own sense of agency with their engagement with the concepts.

CONCLUSIONS

Where are we now in relation to Gruber's concerns about extraordinary moral responsibility and moral creativity? It is clear that, for many

countries in the world, the position of civic education and the development
of moral responsibility generally have been completely transformed since
1983. This transformation has also changed some of the definitions, and
many of the issues, around which moral responsibility was discussed
twenty years ago.

Even without the changes in the former Eastern bloc nations and their
effects on the West, there have been significant developments in civic education. Further, the global issues of the environment, and in a different
way, scientific developments, have made ethical awareness much more a
matter of public debate and accountability. Morality is no longer sidelined;
moral responsibility is on the agenda.

However, in the majority of Western European countries, there is only
a low to moderate expectation of participation—whether conventional or
unconventional. Many former Eastern bloc countries, after the initial energy, now experience disillusion and apathy.

We have a long way to go before these issues are resolved. Efficacy
and appropriate engagement do not come easily. And moral creativity
and extraordinary moral responsibility are, sadly, never likely to be on the
official education agenda—despite the remarkable and rapid transition of
environmentalism from a fringe and radical movement thirty years ago, to
a curricular concern that is a core and solid feature worldwide.

Periods of rapid political and social change generate energy and create
solutions for the formation of a new world, but disillusionment in the face
of setbacks and inertia is inevitable. Perhaps the best that an education
system can do is to be alert to the pressures to retreat into the banal and the
secure. Although the studies I have discussed present largely a broad-brush
picture, it does seem that the tendency to educate for "safe" knowledge
and conventional participation—voting—prevails in many countries. Yet
it is clear that many teachers perceive the need for more praxis, and more
efficacy.

At least if we understand the psychological processes, and the conditions which do, and do not, foster efficacy in the young, we may be able
to move forward in developing educational programs that will give the
next generation these skills and empowerment. We do not yet have the
sort of research material for ordinary moral responsibility that we have for
a small number of extraordinary individuals. We also have, tantalizingly,
in the material discussed in this paper, a strong indication that cultural
processes, particularly at the school and classroom level, are significant
in the development of moral responsibility. Our data on the "normal" is
piecemeal, but a framework is emerging which can guide us in the research
to flesh that out.

REFERENCES

Bell, D. (1993). *Communitarianism and its critics.* Oxford, England: Oxford University Press.

Billig, M. (1992). *Talking of the royal family.* London: Routledge.

Bruner, J. S. (1996). *The culture of education.* Cambridge MA: Harvard University Press.

Call, K.T., Mortimer, J.T., & Shanahan, M.J. (1995). Helpfulness and the development of competence in adolescences. *Child Development,* 6, 129–138.

CBOS (1994). *Adolescents' views about politics.* Warsaw, Poland: Public Opinion Research Center.

Cichowicz, M. (1993). Lyrical model of capitalism. In K. Kosela (Ed.), *To be young in 1992.* Warsaw, Poland: Public Opinion Research Center.

Colby, A. & Kohlberg, L. (1987). *The measurement of moral judgment.* New York: Cambridge University Press.

Colby, A. & Damon, W. (1992). *Some do care, contemporary lives of moral commitment.* New York: The Free Press.

Crick, B. (1998). *Education for citizenship and the teaching of democracy in schools.* London: Qualifications and Curriculum Authority.

Edwards, D. & Mercer, N.M. (1987). *Common knowledge; the development of understanding in the classroom.* London: Methuen.

Flanagan, C.A., Bowes, J.M., Jonsson, B., Csapo, B., & Sheblanova, E. (1998). Ties that bind; correlates of adolescents' civic commitments in seven countries. *Journal of Social Issues,* 54(3), 457–475.

Fogelman, E. (1994). *Conscience and courage.* New York: Doubleday.

Fukuyama, F. (1992). *The end of history and the last man.* New York: Free Press.

Gardner, H. (1999). *The disciplined mind.* New York: Simon & Schuster.

Gardner, H., Damon, W., & Csikszentmihalyi, M. (2001). *Good work; when excellence and ethics meet.* New York: Basic Books.

Gilligan, C. (1982). *In a different voice.* Cambridge, MA: Harvard University Press.

Gruber, H.E. (1989). The evolving systems approach to creative work. In D.B. Wallace & H.E. Gruber (Eds.), *Creative people at work: Twelve cognitive case studies.* New York: Oxford University Press.

Gruber, H.E. (1986). The self-construction of the extraordinary. In R.J. Sternberg & J.E. Davidson (Eds.), *Conceptions of giftedness.* Cambridge, MA: Cambridge University Press.

Gruber, H.E. (1981). *Darwin on man, a psychological study of scientific creativity,* 2nd ed. Chicago: University of Chicago Press.

Hahn, C. (1998). *Becoming political; comparative perspectives on citizenship education.* Albany: State University of New York Press.

Hamilton, S.F. & Fenzel, L.M. (1988). The impact of volunteer experience on adolescent social development. *Journal of Adolescent Research,* 3(1), 65–80.

Harré, R. (1998). *The singular self.* London: Sage.

Harré, R., Muhlhausler, P., & Brockmeier, D. (1999). *Greenspeak.* Thousand Oaks, England: Sage.

Harré, R., & Gillett, G. (1994). *The discursive mind.* London, England: Sage.

Hart, D., Atkins, R., & Ford, D. (1998). Urban America as a context for the Development of moral identity in adolescence. *Journal of Social Issues,* 54(3), 513–530.

Hart, D. & Fegley, S. (1995). Prosocial behavior and caring. *Child Development,* 66, 1346–1359.

Haste, H. (2001). Ambiguity, autonomy and agency; psychological challenges to new competence. In D.S. Rrychen & L.H. Salganic (Eds.), *Defining and selecting key competencies.* Seattle, WA: Hogrefe & Huber, 93–120.

Haste, H. (1996). Communitarianism and the social construction of morality. *Journal of Moral Education*, 25(1), 47–55.

Haste, H.E. (1993). Moral creativity and education for citizenship. *Creativity Research Journal*, 6(1&2), 153–164.

Haste, H. (1990). Moral responsibility and moral commitment; the integration of affect and cognition. In T. Wren (Ed.), *The moral domain*. Cambridge, MA: MIT.

Haste, H. (1989). Everybody's scared but life goes on; coping, defence and action in the face of nuclear threat. *Journal of Adolescence*, 12, 11–26. Press.

Haste, H. (1986). Kohlberg's contribution to political psychology: a positive view. In S. Modgil & C. Modgil (Eds.), *Kohlberg: Consensus and controversy*. Lewes, England: Falmer Press, 337–362.

Haste, H. & Tyrrell, C. (2002). Efficacy and engagement in British adolescents. Paper presented at the annual meeting of the International Society for Political Psychology, Berlin.

Haste, H., Helkama, K., & Markoulis, D. (1998). Morality, wisdom and the lifespan. In A. Demetriou., W. Doise., & C. van Lieshout (Eds.), *Lifespan developmental psychology*. Chichester, England: Wiley, 317–350.

Hekman, S. (1995). *Moral voices, moral selves*. Oxford, England: Polity Press.

Higgins, A. (1991). The Just Community approach to moral education; evolution of the idea and recent findings. In W.M. Kurtines & J.L. Gewirtz (Eds.), *Handbook of moral behavior and development, Vol. 3*, pp. 111–141, Hillsdale, NJ: Erlbaum.

House of Lords Select Committee on Science and Technology (2000). *Report on science and society*. London: The Stationery Office.

Ichilov, O. (1998). (Ed.), *Citizenship and citizenship Education in a changing world*. London: The Woburn Press.

Kaase, M. (1990). Mass participation. In M.K. Jennings & J.W. van Deth (Eds.), *Continuities in political action*. Berlin: de Gruyter, 23–67.

Kahn, P. (1999). *The human relationship with nature*. Cambridge, MA: MIT Press.

Kohlberg, L. & Candee, D. (1984). The relationship of moral judgement to moral action. In W. Kurtines & J. Gewirtz (Eds.), *Morality, moral behavior and moral development*. New York: Wiley, 52–73.

Lenhart, L.A. & Rabiner, D.L. (1995). Social competence in adolescence. *Development and Psychopathology*, 2, 543–561.

Lewis, A. (2002). *Morals, markets and money*. London: Pearson.

Marsh, A. (1977). *Protest and political consciousness*. London: Sage.

Marshall, T.H. (1977). *Class, citizenship and social development*. Chicago: University of Chicago Press.

Morris, B. (1992). Adolescent leaders. *Adolescence*, 27, 173–181.

Noddings, N. (1984). *Caring*. Berkeley: University of California Press.

Paolicchi, P. (1995). Narratives of volunteering. *Journal of Moral Education*, 24 (2), 159–174.

Power, C., Higgins, A., & Kohlberg, L. (1989). *Lawrence Kohlberg's approach to moral education*. New York: Columbia University Press.

Roker, D., Player, K., & Coleman, J. (1999). Exploring adolescent altruism: British young people's involvement in voluntary work and campaigning. In M. Yates & J. Youniss (Eds.), *Roots of civic identity; international perspectives on community service and activism in youth*. Cambridge, England: Cambridge University Press, 56–72.

Rutter, M., Maughan, B., Mortimore, P., & Ouston, J. (1979). *Fifteen thousand hours; secondary schools and their effects on children*. Buckingham, England: Open Books.

School Curriculum Assessment Authority (SCAA). (1996). *National forum for values in education and the community; consultation on values in education and the community.* COM/96/608, School Curriculum Assessment Authority.

Shotter, J. (1993). Becoming someone: Identity and belonging. In N. Coupland & J.F. Nussbaum (Eds.), *Discourse and lifespan identity.* London: Sage.

Taylor, C. (1991). *The ethics of authenticity.* Cambridge, MA: Harvard University Press.

Torney-Purta, J., Lehmann, R., Oswald H., & Schulz, W. (2001). *Citizenship and education in twenty-eight countries: Civic knowledge and engagement at age fourteen.* Amsterdam, The Netherlands: The International Association for the Evaluation of Educational Achievement.

Torney-Purta, J., Schwille, J., & Amadeo, J-A. (Eds.). (1999). *Civic education across countries: Twenty-four national case studies from the IEA Civic Education project.* Amsterdam, The Netherlands: The International Association for the Evaluation of Educational Achievement.

Valdmaa, S. (1999). Identities in Estonia–challenges for citizenship education. In A. Ross (Ed.), *Young citizens in Europe.* London: Children's Identity and Citizenship in Europe.

Van Hoorn, J.L., Komlosi, A., Suchar, E., & Samelson, D. (1999). *Adolescent development and rapid social change.* Albany, NY: SUNY Press.

Wertsch, J. (1998). *Mind as action.* New York: Oxford University Press.

Yates, M. & Youniss, J. (1999). *Roots of civic identity: international perspectives on community service and activism in youth.* Cambridge, England: Cambridge University Press.

Youniss, J., McLellan, J.A. & Yates, M. (1997). What we know about engendering civic identity. *American Behavioral Scientist, 40,* 620–631.

INDEX

169